SCOTTISH-AMERICAN
GRAVESTONES
1700–1900

by
David Dobson

CLEARFIELD

Printed for
Clearfield Company, Inc. by
Genealogical Publishing Co., Inc.
Baltimore, Maryland
1998

Reprinted for
Clearfield Company, Inc. by
Genealogical Publishing Co., Inc.
Baltimore, Maryland
2000, 2003

International Standard Book Number: 0-8063-4803-8

Made in the United States of America

INTRODUCTION

Gravestones and monumental inscriptions contain a wealth of information for the family historian. This primary source of data is of particular importance to Scottish genealogists as the Old Parish Registers of the Church of Scotland concentrate on baptism and marriage and contain little on burials. Gravestone inscriptions thus provide an almost unique source for deaths prior to 1855 in Scotland and for information on Scots dying overseas before that date. After 1855 there are statutory records of births, marriages and deaths in Scotland. The only other major sources of such information lie in the obituary pages of the press or in the various Registers of Testaments.

Graveyards have attracted the attention of antiquarians for centuries. As early as 1704 Robert Monteith published his <u>Theatre of Mortality</u> listing inscriptions from burial grounds in Edinburgh. During the nineteenth century James Brown published his <u>Epitaphs and Monumental Inscriptions on Greyfriars Churchyard</u> in 1867 while Charles Rogers published his <u>Monuments and Monumental Inscriptions</u> in 1872. More recently various family history societies, especially the Scottish Genealogy Society and the Aberdeen Family History Society, have been actively recording the inscriptions. The urgency of the work results from the fact that many stones are crumbling away, while others have been subject to vandalism or to destruction by local authorities clearing graveyards prior to 'development.'

Much of the inscriptions have now been published by the societies concerned, but the project is as yet incomplete. This book is based on both published and unpublished material. It should be noted that this is not an exhaustive list as some researchers did not note anything dated after 1855 while others took a more comprehensive approach. Those wishing to learn more about the subject are recommended to read Betty Willsher's <u>Understanding Scottish Graveyards</u> [Edinburgh, 1995].

David Dobson

SCOTTISH - AMERICAN

GRAVESTONES

1700 -1900

ADAM, DAVID, born 1832, son of Thomas Adam and Ellen Adam,
   died in Morris City, Manitoba, 15.1.1886. [Lintrathen g/s]
ADAM, PETER, a mason on Fox Island, son of George Adam {1808-
   1881} and Isabella Reid {1810-1880}, died 17.9.1872, buried in
   Palmer, Massachusetts. [Monymusk g/s]
ADAMSON, CHARLES, born 1829, died at Cape Florida 11.12.1870.
   [Arbroath Abbey g/s]
ADAMSON, JAMES, born 1825, son of Alexander Adamson and Jane
   Hastie, died in Grouse Island, America, 12.6.1847.
   [St Monance g/s]
ADAMSON, ROBERT, born 1821, son of Archibald Adamson {1793-
   1858} and Jane Arthur {1794-1841}, died in Illinois 3.2.1873.
   [Bathgate, Kirkton, g/s]
AIKMAN, PETER, born 1819, son of George Aikman and Alison
   MacKay, died in New York 15.9.1883.
   [Edinburgh, St Cuthbert's g/s]
AINSLIE, ROBERT GORDON, born 18.6.1843, son of Robert Forrest
   Ainslie {1811-1862}, died 13.6.1848 in Hamilton, Canada West.
   [Rothesay g/s]
AINSLIE, WILLIAM ALLAN, born 9.1.1839, son of Robert F.
   Ainslie {1811-1862}, died 2.3.1840 in Hamilton, Canada West.
   [Rothesay g/s]
AIRD, ROBERT, born 1804, son of Thomas Aird and Elizabeth
   Young, died in Quebec 23.8.1834. [Alloway g/s]
AIRTH, MARY, died in Montreal 19.2.1882. [Arbroath Abbey g/s]

1

AITCHISON, WILLIAM ALEXANDER, born 20.3.1834, son of
Archibald Aitchison and Anne Ferguson Jamieson, Lieutenant of
the 59th Regiment of Virginia Volunteers, Confederate States
Army, died in Richmond, Virginia, 26.1.1865.
[Edinburgh, St Cuthbert's, g/s]

AITKEN, PETER, born 1852, died in Boston, USA, 28.6.1887.
[Torpichen g/s]

ALEXANDER, DAVID GRAY, born 1812, son Robert Alexander,
died in Virginia City, California, 30.7.1862. [Ayton g/s]

ALEXANDER, EDWARD MAYNE, born in Halifax, Nova Scotia,
16.12.1840, died in St Leonard's 1.8.1916. [Logie, Stirling, g/s]

ALEXANDER, FRANCIS, born in Toull 20.11.1806, died in
Tuscaloosa, Alabama, 20.8.1856. [Buittle g/s]

ALEXANDER, MARGARET, born 1791, daughter of John Shaw
Alexander, wife of John Johnston, died in Geneva, Ontario
County, New York, 30.8.1854. [Dalry g/s]

ALLAN, GEORGE, born 1854, son of Alexander Allan and Anne
Fraser, died in Thamesford, USA, 9.4.1883. [Dornoch g/s]

ALLAN, JAMES, born 1860, son of James Allan {1820-1901} and
Janet Barr {1819-1884}, died in Yonkers, New York, 7.2.1869.
[Johnstone g/s]

ALLAN, JAMES GLEN, born 1815, died in Nova Scotia 12.1.1886.
[Old Calton, Edinburgh, g/s]

ALLAN, JOHN, born 1839, son of Alexander Allan and Anne Fraser,
died in Cincinatti, USA, 23.9.1886. [Dornoch g/s]

ALLAN, MARY, born 1863, daughter of Alexander Allan and Isabella
Gray, died in USA 14.11.1898. [Dyce g/s]

ALLAN, PETER, born 1861, son of Alexander Allan and Isabella
Gray, died in USA 15.6.1892. [Dyce g/s]

ALLAN, ROBERT, born 1805, son of Robert Allan {1778-1858} and
Elizabeth Lindsay {1779-1842}, died in New Orleans 17.6.1830.
[Dundee, Constitution Road, g/s]

ALLISON, JAMES, born 1856, son of John Allison and Jessie Smith,
died in New York 19.1.1890. [St Clement's, Aberdeen, g/s]

AMOS, MARGARET, born 1812, daughter of Andrew Amos {1775-
1855} and Jane Oliver {1781-1832}, died in Troy, USA,
2.10.1837. [Libberton, Edinburgh, g/s]

ANDERSON, ALEXANDER, born 1810, son of John Anderson and
Ann White, died in New York 18.12.1845. [Montrose g/s]
ANDERSON, ANNE, born 1792, daughter of Laurence Anderson and
Jane Watson, died in New York 24.11.1825. [St Andrews g/s]
ANDERSON, CHARLES ENVERDALE, born 1838, sometime
Provost of Coupar Angus, died in New York 2.1.1902.
[Coupar Angus g/s]
ANDERSON, GEORGE, born 1798, son of George Anderson and
Agnes Kerr, died in New Orleans 7.10.1827. [Inverkeiller g/s]
ANDERSON, GEORGE, born 1827, son of George Anderson and
Euphemia Scott, died in Cincinatti, USA, 11.1854.
[Auchterhouse g/s]
ANDERSON, JAMES, born 1797, son of Laurence Anderson and Jane
Watson, died in Newark, USA, 12.4.1830. [St Andrews g/s]
ANDERSON, JAMES, born 1844, died in New York 1.11.1868.
[Arbroath Abbey g/s]
ANDERSON, JOHN, born 1810, son of John Anderson and Isabella
Anderson, died in Kingston, Canada West, 2.1859. [Swinton g/s]
ANDERSON, JOHN, born 1790, son of James Anderson and Margaret
Miller, died in Halifax, North America, 17.7.1810.
[Kilrenny g/s]
ANDERSON, JOHN DAVID, born 1819, died in Bermuda 31.7.1857.
[Burntisland g/s]
ANDERSON, MARGARET, born 1840, wife of Lachlan Halliburton,
died in Washington, D.C., 16.4.1909. [Dundee, Western, g/s]
ANDERSON, ROBERT MUNRO, son of John Anderson {1789-1840}
and Mary Ross {1806-1871}, died in New York.
[Kincardine, Wester Ross, g/s]
ANDERSON, THOMAS, born 1795, son of George Anderson and
Agnes Kerr, died in New Orleans 1.8.1835. [Inverkeillor g/s]
ANDERSON, THOMAS BROWN, son of Peter Anderson, a merchant
who died 1820, and Magdalene Anderson, a merchant in
Montreal. [Buccleuch g/s]
ANDREW, JOHN MCADAM, born 16.9.1807, son of John Anderson
and Jean McAdam, died in New York 24.5.1835.
[Kilmarnock g/s]
ANDREWS, ROBERT, born 1858, son of William Andrews and Mary
Milroy, died in Winnipeg 27.10.1882. [Colmonell g/s]

ANGUS, GEORGE, born 1830, son of John Angus and Mary Sime, died in America 4.4.1869. [Cupar g/s]

ANTON, GEORGE MILLAR, born 1872, son of James Anton, a farmer in Wester Kinloch, {1818-1891} and Mary Bullions {1837-1873}, died in Duluth, Minnesota, 1.7.1901. [Clunie g/s]

ARCHER, JAMES, born 1801, son of Andrew Archer, a minister, died in New Lebanon, North America, 1825. [Tealing g/s]

ARKLEY, EVELYN, daughter of Patrick Arkley and Julia C Arkley, died in Lyn, USA, 14.8.1869. [Murroes g/s]

ARMOUR, JEAN, daughter of Robert Armour, settled in Montreal by 1877. [Kilmarnock g/s]

ARMSTRONG, JAMES, born 1797, son of Theodore Armstrong and Agnes Harris, died in Miramachi 15.7.1828. [Colvend g/s]

ARMSTRONG, MARY, born 1799, daughter of George Armstrong and Janet Haig, died in America 22.1.1856. [Fogo g/s]

ARMSTRONG, ROBERT, born 1873, died in Milwaukee 14.11.1891. [Muthill g/s]

ARNOTT, WILLIAM, born 1824, son of Alexander Arnott and Jane Lindsay, died in New Jersey City 3.10.1894. [Brechin Cathedral g/s]

ARNOT, WILLIAM WILSON, born 4.8.1822, son of William Arnot {1795-1836} a blacksmith, and Margaret Campbell {179..-1869}, died in Hamilton, Canada West, 20.3.1853. [South Leith g/s]

ARROL, JANET, daughter of Thomas Arrol {1816-1891} and Agnes Hodgart {1810-1889}, wife of John Hunter, died in Montreal 1890. [Paisley Woodside g/s]

ARTHUR, Captain JAMES, born 1798, son of .... Arthur and Elizabeth Herald {1768-1841}, died in New York 4.1838. [Dundee, Howff, g/s]

AULD, JAMES, son of Hugh Auld {1781-1844} and Margaret King {1782-1851}, died in Chicago 9.11.1883. [Crosbie, Ayrshire, g/s]

BAIN, DAVID, born 1853, son of Andrew Bain {1806-1871} a shipbuilder in Dundee, and Christian Dorward {1815-1888}, died in Brooklyn, New York, 30.5.1889. [Dundee, Eastern Necropolis, g/s]

BAIN, KENNETH, born 1873, son of Peter Bain and Christine Henderson, died in Kamloops, Vancouver, 26.7.1896.

[Latheron Old g/s]
BAIN, ROBERT, born 1759, son of Archibald Bain, {1715-1801}, a
  farmer in Row parish, and Jane Taylor, {1717-1808}, a merchant
  in Norfolk, Virginia, died 21.8.1792. [Gourock g/s]
BAIN, WILLIAMINA, born 1858, wife of John Clyne, died in Auburn,
  USA, 12.5.1884. [Keiss g/s]
BALFOUR, JAMES, born 1836, son of William Balfour and Mary
  Duncan, died in America 30.7.1875. [Kilrenny g/s]
BALLANTYNE, ISABELLA, died in North America 17.1.1861.
  [Perth, Greyfriars, g/s]
BALLANTYNE, JAMES BURN, born 1829, died in Texas 4.12.1877.
  [Edinburgh, St Cuthbert's, g/s]
BALLENDINE, MARGARET CAMERON, born 1841, daughter of
  John Ballendine jr., died in Sault Sainte Marie, Canada, 6.1843.
  [Edinburgh, New Calton, g/s]
BANCKS, MARY JANE, born 1820, late of Bowdley, Coburg, Upper
  Canada, died 8.7.1840. [Rothesay g/s]
BANKS, HELEN, born 1813, daughter of William Banks {1781-1839}
  and Ann Mitchell {1782-1852}, wife of C.J.Farrar, died in
  Pennsylvania 5.4.1850. [Buccleuch g/s]
BARCLAY, ALEXANDER, MD, born 1810, died in Newburgh, New
  York, 1.5.1889. [St Clement's, Aberdeen, g/s]
BARBER, THOMAS, born 1830, son of Thomas Barber and Madelina
  McLeod, died in Andersonville, Georgia, 9.9.1864. [Bellie g/s]
BARRON, JOHN, born 1810, son of John Barron {1765-1852} a
  watchmaker and Ann Allan, died in New York 30.8.1851.
  [Old Aberdeen g/s]
BARRON, WILLIAM, born 1836, son of Thomas Barron and
  Catherine Taylor, died in St Louis, USA, 17.9.1878. [Alyth g/s]
BAYNE, JAMES, born 1804, minister of Princes Street Church,
  Pictou, Nova Scotia, died 9.12.1866. [Dunbar g/s]
BAYNE, JANET, daughter of James Bayne {1822-1898} and Ann
  McKenzie {died 1909}, wife of William Kirton, died in Calgary,
  Alberta, 8.4.1901. [Dunblane g/s]
BAYNE, THOMAS, born in East Barns 17.2.1819, died in Halifax,
  Nova Scotia, 30.9.1890. [Dunbar g/s]
BEATTIE, FRANCIS, born 1796, son of Francis Beattie and Elizabeth
  Brown, died in Port Hope, Upper Canada, 29.9.1828.

5

[Dumfries g/s]

BECK, WILLIAM, son of James Beck and Sophia Bell, died in Quebec aged 29. [Dumfries g/s]

BEGG, ARCHIBALD, born 1777, son of Hugh Begg and Margaret Taylor, died in America 4.1816. [Lesmahagow g/s]

BEGG, HUGH, born 1776, son of Hugh Begg and Margaret Taylot, died in America 11.1806. [Lesmahagow g/s]

BELL, CATHERINE, born 1817, wife of William Roy, died in New Orleans 27.5.1858. [Cupar g/s]

BELL, JAMES, born 1809, son of David Bell and Elizabeth Hunter, died in New York 28.8.1859, buried in Greenwood Cemetery. [Duns g/s]

BELL, JOHN, born 1826, son of Andrew Bell, a merchant in St Louis, Missouri, died 30.3.1860. [Cockburnspath g/s]

BENSON, WILLIAM, born 1845, son of Robert Benson, died in New York 18.7.1874. [Greenock g/s]

BENTLEY, ANTONIA, born 1781, widow of Paul Weston MD in Charleston, South Carolina, died in Portobello 16.12.1857. [Edinburgh, Greyfriars, g/s]

BERWICK, DAVID, born 1829, son of David Berwick and Jean Berwick, died in Oakland, California, 12.2.1896. [St Andrews g/s]

BIGGAR, GEORGE, born 1862, son of James Biggar {1830-1898} and Elizabeth Bryden {1831-1910}, died in New York 22.11.1898, buried in Macphelah Cemetery, New Jersey. [Ettrick g/s]

BIRRELL, EBENEZER, born 1801, son of John Birrell and Christine Arnott, died in Maple Hall, Canada, 27.2.1888. [Portmoak g/s]

BLACK, ANGUS, born 1834, son of James Black {1807-1852} and Isabel McBride {1810-1881}, died in Winnipeg 8.1882. [Kilbride, Arran, g/s]

BLACK, GEORGE, son of Thomas Black and Mary Dunbar {1800-1855}, died in Upper Canada 17.12.18.. aged 35. [Dyke g/s]

BLACK, JAMES, son of Robert Black {died 1790} and Rachel Tay {died 1798}, settled in Philadelphia. [Edinburgh, St Cuthbert's, g/s]

BLACK, JAMES, born 1769, late of Philadelphia, died in Edinburgh 24.3.1843, widow Elliot Miller died 2.9.1848. [Edinburgh, New Calton, g/s]

BLACK, JOHN, born 1762, a merchant in Halifax, Nova Scotia, and
Member of HM Council of Nova Scotia, died in Aberdeen
4.9.1823. [New Machar g/s]
BLACK, JOHN, [born 11.3.1817, late of the Hudson Bay Company,
died 3.2.1879. [St Andrews g/s]
BLACK, JOHN, born 1829, son of Adam Black and Helen Elliot, died
in America 17.7.1859. [Preston, Berwickshire, g/s]
BLAIR, JOHN, born 1790, son of James Blair and Jean Dunlop, died
in America 1820. [Stewarton g/s]
BLAKIE, JANE, born 1736, wife of William Spiden a merchant in
Bowden, died in Kentucky 1819. [Bewlie g/s]
BLAIKIE, GEORGE, born 1782, son of Andrew Blaikie and Jane
Currie, died in Chicago 1.8.1851. [Bewlie g/s]
BLAIKIE, JAMES, born 1827, son of Andrew Blaikie and Jane Currie,
died in St John's, Newfoundland, 2.6.1888. [Bewlie g/s]
BOGLE, JAMES, born 1868, son of Thomas Bogle and Elizabeth
Jamieson Brown, died in Albany, New York, 24.6.1913, buried
in Bethell, Vermont. [Roberton g/s]
BONELLA, ANN, daughter of John Bonella and Margaret Fernie, died
in Kansas 19.9.1859. [Leuchars g/s]
BORROMAN, ALEXANDER, born 1820, son of Robert Borroman
{1784-} and Elizabeth Stevenson {1789-1841}, died in Montreal
17.12.1884. [Edinburgh, Greyfriars, g/s]
BORTHWICK, CHARLES, born 1840, son of James Borthwick and
Mary Milne, died in San Francisco 12.8.1881.
[Arbroath Abbey g/s]
BORTHWICK, WILLIAM, born 1846, son of James Borthwick and
Mary Milne, died in Berkeley, California, 27.9.1921.
[Arbroath Abbey g/s]
BOYD, BEATRICE, daughter of Richard Boyd and Ann Butler {died
6.5.1860}, buried in Wilmington, North Carolina. [Dalmeny g/s]
BOYD, HELEN, born 1833, wife of James Bryden, died in Piston,
Pennsylvania, 3.4.1861. [Alloway g/s]
BOYD, JAMES, son of Richard Boyd and Ann Butler {died 6.5.1860},
buried in Wilmington, North Carolina. [Dalmeny g/s]
BOYD, JOHN, born 1834, son of Charles Boyd {1793-1844} and Jane
Young {1799-1880}, died at the Battle of Bull Run, USA,
21.7.1861. [Kirkliston g/s]

BOYD, PHILIP, son of Richard Boyd and Ann Butler {died 6.5.1860}, buried in Wilmington, North Carolina. [Dalmeny g/s]

BOYD, THOMAS WARDLAW, born 14.7.1850, son of Ebemezer Boyd and Mary Paul, died in New York 2.4.1886. [Edinburgh, Old Calton, g/s]

BOYD, WILLIAM, born 1874, son of William Boyd and Catherine Graham, died in Norwich, Connecticut, 18.8.1919, buried in East London. [Dunbarton, Bridgend, g/s]

BRAND, JAMES MCQUEEN, son of James Brand {1781-1840} and Jean McQueen, settled in New York. [Dumfries g/s]

BRINE, ELIZABETH, born 1810 in St John, Newfoundland, wife of Kenneth McLea, died in Greenock 17.8.1854. [Greenock g/s]

BROAD, JOHN W., born 1826, son of Michael Broad and Helen Walker, died in Paris, Texas, 1.1877. [Kirkhope g/s]

BRODIE, ALEXANDER, son of Thomas Brodie and Jean Middlemiss {1781-1814}, settled in Baltimore, Maryland, before 1847. [Fishwick g/s]

BRODIE, JOHN, son of Thomas Brodie and Jean Middlemiss {1781-1814}, settled in Baltimore, Maryland, before 1847. [Fishwick g/s]

BROWN, AGNES, born 1801, daughter of Mackenzie Brown and Elizabeth Jamieson, died in America 19.10.1842. [Dolphinton g/s]

BROWN, ALEXANDER, born 1832, son of Peter Brown {1819-1887} and Matilda ... {1820-1902}, died in Washington, USA, 26.3.1866. [Greenock g/s]

BROWN, ALEXANDER, born 1794, died in Milton, Ontario, 13.11.1876. [Senwick g/s]

BROWN, ANDREW, born 1763, a minister in Halifax, Nova Scotia, died in Edinburgh 19.2.1834. [Edinburgh, Greyfriars, g/s]

BROWN, DANIEL, born in North America 1822, son of William Brown of the Hudson Bay Company and Barbara Muir, died in Kilmaurs 9.11.1829. [Kilmaurs g/s]

BROWN, DAVID LESLIE, born 1826, died at Pondo Bay, Davis Strait, 29.7.1881. [Arbroath Abbey g/s]

BROWN, GEORGE, born 1832, son of Charles Brown and Mary Kinnear, died in Brooklyn 24.2.1874. [Ferry Port on Craig g/s]

8

BROWN, JAMES, born 15.3.1835, son of James Brown, died in Lake Superior 28.12.1861. [Galston g/s]

BROWN JESSE, son of Jesse Brown, master of the American ship London of Newberryport, died in the wreck of the above ship off North Ronaldsay 3.10.1831. [North Ronaldsay g/s]

BROWN, JOHN, born 1828, son of John Brown {1786-1860} and Elizabeth Law {1789-1850}, died in New York 9.6.1852. [Edinburgh, Grange, g/s]

BROWN, JOHN, born 1843, son of James Brown and Janet Gardner, died in Namino, British Columbia, 12.4.1886. [St Monance g/s]

BROWN, THOMAS, born 1845, grandson of Thomas Brown {1753-1835} and Agnes Sinclair {1782-1841}, a farmer in Petite Cote, Montreal, died in Broughton 11.2.1892. [Coulter g/s]

BROWN, WILLIAM, a employee of the Hudson Bay Company, died before 1829. [Kilmaurs g/s]

BROWN, WILLIAM, born 1735, Colonel and Collector of New York, died 1810. [Eccles g/s]

BROWN, WILLIAM, born 1829, son of James Brown and Janet Gardner, died in New York 21.6.1866. [St Monance g/s]

BROWN, WILLIAM, son of William Brown {1810-1886} and Mary Methven {died 1870}, settled in Hoboken, New Jersey. [Dunbar g/s]

BROWN, WILLIAM, born 1822, son of Peter Brown {1819-1887} and Matilda ... {1820-1902}, a mason, died in Philadelphia 4.3.1858. [Greenock g/s]

BRUCE, JAMES, born 18.6.1846, son of John Bruce and Elizabeth Smith, died in Nashville, USA, 30.6.1882. [Fettercairn g/s]

BRUCE, JOHN, born 1845, son of George Bruce and Elizabeth Gould, died in Quebec 5.12.1871. [Arbroath g/s]

BRUCE, LAURENCE, born 1836, died in Mexico 21.2.1904. [Cargill g/s]

BRUCE, WILLIAM M., born 1844, died in Warrenburg, USA, 17.3.1892. [Cargill g/s]

BRUCE, WILLIAM ANDREW, born 1854, son of John Bruce {1825-1895} and Christian Ritchie {1829-1871}, died in Harford, California, 12.10.1896. [Monymusk g/s]

BRYCE, JOHN, son of Thomas Bryce {1758-1837} and Agnes Brown {1763-1840}, died in Toronto aged 89. [Symington g/s]

BRYDEN, DAVID, son of Adam Bryden {1766-1850} and Margaret
   Armstrong {1773-1842}, settled in Canada 1847.
   [St Mary's, Selkirk, g/s]
BRYDEN, THOMAS, born 1848, son of Thomas Bryden and Margaret
   Hunter, died in Shreveport, Louisiana, 1.7.1871.
   [Kirkmichael g/s]
BRYMER, JOHN FAIRLIE, born 1815, son of Alexander Brymer and
   Elizabeth Fairlie, died in Quebec 7.6.1829. [Greenock g/s]
BUIST, HENRY, born 1804, son of Henry Buist and Rachel
   Robertson, died in Canada 19.12.1876. [Strathmiglo g/s]
BURN, HANNAH KING, wife of Daniel McIntosh a merchant, died in
   St John, New Brunswick, 9.6.1828.
   [Edinburgh, St Cuthbert's, g/s]
BURN, JAMES, born 1782, son of Alexander Burn and Margaret
   Edward, settled in St John, New Brunswick. [Fetteresso g/s]
BURN, JOHN, born 1733, Member of HM Council of South Carolina,
   died 29.12.1776. [Inveresk g/s]
BURN, JOHN, born 1786, son of Alexander Burn and Margaret
   Edward, settled in St John, New Brunswick. [Fetteresso g/s]
BURNESS, ALEXANDER LOW, born 1844, son of Alexander
   Burness and Ann Falconer, died in Winnipeg, Manitoba,
   19.1.1883. [Edzell g/s]
BURNESS, HENRY, born 1819, a baker, died in Toronto 29.11.1877.
   [Montrose, Episcopal, g/s]
BUTLER, MARY, born in Boston, North America, 1763, daughter of
   William Butler and Mary Butler, wife of David Laird, died in
   Strathmartine 1797. [Strathmartine g/s]
CAIRNCROSS, ROBERT GRIEVE, born 24.4.1834, son of Robert
   Cairncross and Janet Gowans, died in Central Park West, New
   York City 22.5.1899. [Brechin Cathedral g/s]
CAIRNS, MARY, wife of William Ewing, died 20.8.1889, buried in
   Montreal. [Stirling g/s]
CALDER. JEAN, born 1844, daughter of Alexander Calder and
   Catherine Murray, died in Kentucky 1908. [Creich g/s]
CAMERON, ALEXANDER, son of John Cameron {1760-1836} and
   Janet Paxton {1767-1851}, died at Ardoise Hill, Nova Scotia,
   1.7.1866. [Chirnside g/s]

CAMERON, GEORGE, son of James Cameron {1775-1843} and
Margaret Webster {1791-1861}, died in Mexico 1867.
[Dundee, Constitution Road, g/s]

CAMERON, GILBERT, born 1809, son of Douglas Cameron {1780-
1854} and Jean Sayers {1786-1865}, a builder, late of
Washington, USA, died 6.11.1866. [Greenock, Inverkip St., g/s]

CAMERON, HECTOR, born 1853, son of Donald Cameron and Anne
Gordon, died in New York 1897. [Dornoch g/s]

CAMERON, HUGH, born 8.10.1852, son of Hugh Cameron and Jean
Fairlie, died in Omaha 2.9.1916. [Greenock g/s]

CAMERON, HUGH PERCY, born 1817, son of Alexander Cameron
{1776-1831} and Mary Davidson {1779-1858}, died in
Charleston, South Carolina, 18.9.1854. [Little Dunkeld g/s]

CAMERON, Dr JAMES, son of James Cameron {1752-1832} and
Magdalene Gordon {1757-1830}, settled in New York.
[Milnathort g/s]

CAMPBELL, ARCHIBALD, born 1746, formerly a Captain of the
South Carolina Dragoons, died 8.4.1834. [Inveraray g/s]

CAMPBELL, ARCHIBALD, born 1813, son of Archibald Campbell, a
sawyer, and Margaret Watt, died in New Orleans 5.10.1839.
[Perth, Greyfriars, g/s]

CAMPBELL, COLIN C., in Brooklyn, New York, son of Norman
Campbell {died 1868} and Ann McIver {1795-1860}.
[Dingwall, St Clement's, g/s]

CAMPBELL, Sir DONALD, born 1800, Lieutenant Governor of
Prince Edward Island, died 10.10.1850.
[Dunstaffnage Chapel g/s]

CAMPBELL, DONALD, born 1847, son of Charles Campbell and Ann
Campbell, died in America 1874. [Durness g/s]

CAMPBELL, ELIZABETH, born 1810, daughter of David Campbell
and Mary Porter, died in New Orleans 1.9.1838. [Buittle g/s]

CAMPBELL, HUGH PERCY, born 1817 son of Alexander Campbell
{1776-1831} and Mary Davidson {1779-1858}, died in
Charleston, South Carolina, 18.9.1854. [Little Dunkeld g/s]

CAMPBELL, Mrs ISABELLA, born 1828, daughter of William
Robertson {1802-1894} and Elizabeth Sutherland {1799-1851},
died in Grimsby, Canada West, 19.11.1869. [Bellie g/s]

CAMPBELL, JAMES, son of Alexander Campbell in Loderoifr {1740-1791}, died in Canada 1828. [Shian Kenmore g/s]

CAMPBELL, JAMES, son of William Campbell {1770-1854} and Elizabeth Frant {1769-1851}, settled in Toronto.
[Edinburgh, Greyfriars, g/s]

CAMPBELL, JANE, daughter of Archibald Campbell {1790-1838} and Jean Graham {1789-1854}, died in Nashville, Tennessee, 19.5.1849. [Denny g/s]

CAMPBELL, JEAN, born 1788, daughter of David Campbell and Janet McNish, died in Delaware City, USA, 13.11.1853.
[Balmaghie g/s]

CAMPBELL, JOHN, born 1642, "banished to America for Christ's Cause in 1683 but by Providence he returned in 1685 and died 8.1721" [Barr g/s]

CAMPBELL, JOHN, son of John McLeod Campbell and Mary Jenkins, died in Middletown, New York, 5.3.1902.
[Rosneath g/s]

CAMPBELL, JOHN R., son of Andrew Campbell {1828-1888} and Sophia Rennick {1835-1910}, died in America 13.2.1909.
[Pollockshaws g/s]

CAMPBELL, LACHLAN, born 1842, son of Duncan Campbell {1805-1872} and Ann McLeod {1803-1883}, died in Galveston, Texas, 11.10.1867. [Greenock g/s]

CAMPBELL, MARGARET, born 1846, daughter of Alexander Campbell and Agnes Reddoch, died in America 23.3.1875.
[Tulliallan g/s]

CAMPBELL, MURDOCH, son of John Campbell {1720-1805} and Margaret McLeod, died in America. [Dunvegan g/s]

CAMPBELL, NORMAN, born in Gairloch, 'sometime in Brooklyn, New York,' died in Dingwall 4.12.1868.
[Dingwall, St Clement's, g/s]

CAMPBELL, WALTER, born 1745, Captain of the Prince of Wales' American Regiment of Foot, died in Perth 18.5.1823, his wife Nancy de Weber, born 1774, died in Dunkeld 9.9.1828.
[Perth Greyfriars g/s]

CAMPBELL, WILLIAM, born 1796, son of William Campbell {1763-1816} and Jane Herron {1752-1835}, died in New York 6.1850.
[Crossmichael g/s]

CAMPBELL, WILLIAM, son of William Campbell {1805-1864} and
Ann Whyte {1809-1884}, died in America. [Durness g/s]

CAMPBELL, WILLIAM, born 1883, son of Charles Campbell and
Robina Mackay, died in Canada 2.11.1906. [Durness g/s]

CARMICHAEL, LAWRENCE, son of Robert Carmichael {1771-
1832} and Janet Dougall {1772-1840}, died in America.
[Milnathort g/s]

CARMICHAEL, ROBERT, born 1816, son of D. Carmichael and
Mary Morrison, died in Kingston, North America, 22.8.1849.
[Oban g/s]

CARNEGIE, CHARLES, born 1840, son of Charles Carnegie and
Sophia Bell, died 9.4.1905, buried in Puebla, Mexico.
[Forfar g/s]

CARNEGIE, JAMES SOUTAR, born 1847, son of Charles Carnegie
and Sophia Bell, died 8.9.1915, buried in Puebla, Mexico.
[Forfar g/s]

CARNOCHAN, SAMUEL, born 1785, son of James Carnochan and
Sarah Houstoun, died in Goderich, Ontario, 5.3.1859.
[Anwoth g/s]

CARRUTHERS, AGNES ROBB, born 1826, daughter of John
Carruthers and Agnes Hamilton, died in Toronto 13.3.1860.
[Kilmarnock, St Andrew's, g/s]

CATTENACH, PETER LORIMER, born 5.8.1879, son of Peter
Lorimer Cattenach and Jane Bladworth Hardie, died 23.9.1905 in
St Louis, USA. [Edinburgh, St Cuthbert's, g/s]

CHALMERS, PETER, born 1844, son of Peter Chalmers and Helen
Spence, died in San Antonio, Texas, 26.4.1879. [Dron g/s]

CHALMERS, WOLSELEY, born 31.10.1876, son of Patrick Chalmers
and Ellen ....., died in Santa Cruz, Mexico, 27.7.1914.
[Aberlemno g/s]

CHAPMAN, SAMUEL, born 1779, son of James Chapman and Jane
..., died in Charleston, North Carolina, (sic), 8.9.1806.
[Carmichael g/s]

CHESNEY, MARGARET P., born 1849, daughter of John Chesney
and Jessie McCord, wife of John S. Findlay, died in Chicago
8.12.1910. [Whithorn g/s]

CHISHOLM, DONALD, born 1853, son of John Chisholm farmer in Invercannich and Anne Chisholm, died in Del Norte, Colorado, 24.3.1917. [Clachan Comair, Kerrow, g/s]

CHISHOLM, HUGH, in Portland, Maine, 1885, grandson of Colin Chisholm of Fanellan, {died 1862}, and Isabel McConnel, {died in Kerrow 1816}. [Clachan Comair, Kerrow, g/s]

CHISHOLM, PETER, born 1845, son of Peter Chisholm {1809-1880} and Margaret Ross {1805-1905}, died in San Francisco 4.6.1876. [Bowmore, Islay, g/s[

CHISHOLM, WILLIAM, born 1843, son of Donald Chisholm and Isabel Murray, died in Boston, USA, 26.1.1911. [Creich g/s]

CHRISTIE, ALEXANDER, born 1830, son of John Christie {1795-1840} a maltster in Stirling, and Janet Tower {1795-1891}, 'late of New York', died 8.8.1875. [Stirling, Holy Rude, g/s]

CLARK, HARRY, born 1842, son of Harry Clark and Elizabeth Cook, died in USA 1.6.1898. [Auchendoir g/s]

CLARKE, ISABELLA MACOMB, born 6.1809, daughter of Thomas Clarke in New Jersey, wife of Rupert John Cochrane in Halifax, Nova Scotia, died 3.9.1851. [Edinburgh, St John's, g/s]

CLARK, JAMES ALEXANDER, born 4.5.1868, son of James Clark {1821-1881} and Jane MacArthur {1829-1893}, died at Colorado Springs, USA, 8.1893. [Paisley, Woodside, g/s]

CLARK, JOHN, born 1779, son of ... Clark and Margaret Scott, settled in Louisiana, died in Maxwelltown 9.4.1866. [Dumfries g/s]

CLARK, JOHN, son of William Clark in Creebridge, settled in New Orleans 18.. [Monigaff g/s]

CLARK, JOHN ALEXANDER, born 4.5.1863, son of James Clark and Jane McArthur, died in Colorado Springs, USA, 8.1893. [Paisley, Woodside, g/s]

CLAYTON, Captain JAMES, born 1781, died in Miramachi, Nova Scotia, 18.5.1818. [Banff g/s]

CLUNAS, ELIZABETH WIRT RANDALL or, born 1828, wife of James Clunas, daughter of Judge Thomas Randall, Tallahassie, Florida, granddaughter of William Wirt, Attorney General of USA 1817-1829, died in Cawdor Place, Nairn, 3.10.1863. [Wardlaw g/s]

14

CLUNAS, GEORGE JOHN, born 1856, MD PhD, died in
Jacksonville, Florida, 4.2.1886. [Wardlaw g/s]

CLUNAS, JAMES, born 1809, son of William Clunas and Janet
Mackay, late in New Orleans, died in Nairn 2.1.1888.
[Wardlaw g/s]

CLUNAS, JOHN, born 1822, son of William Clunas, farmer in Milton
of Leys, Inverness, and Janet Mackay, died in New Orleans
10.9.1886. [Wardlaw g/s]

COATES, ADAM, born 2.4.1825, son of Gilbert Coates and Jane
Kennan, died in USA 23.8.1892. [Balmaghie g/s]

COCHRANE, ALEXANDER, born 1855, son of James Cochrane and
Janet Gemmel, died in California 6.12.1891. [Balmaghie g/s]

COCHRANE, DUNCAN, born 1797, son of Alexander Cochrane and
Christian MacFarlane, died in New York 3.6.1827.
[Dunbarton g/s]

COCHRANE, JAMES, born 1850, son of David Cochrane {1806-
1853} and Agnes Langlands {1810-1892}, died in Brooklyn,
New York, 3.10.1888. [Dundee, Eastern Necropolis, g/s]

COCHRANE, RUPERT JOHN, born 1801, Halifax, Nova Scotia, died
in London 28.6.1851, buried in Battersea.
[Edinburgh, St Cuthbert's, g/s]

COCHRANE, WILLIAM, born 1784, son of William Cochrane and
Agnes, died in the St Lawrence River, Canada, 31.8.1803.
[Inverkip g/s]

COLLIE, HELEN S., born 1856, died 1930, buried in Boston,
Massachusetts. [Brechin Cathedral g/s]

COLLISON, GEORGE, son of Alexander Collison {1779-1819} and
Agnes Buchan {1781-1851}, settled in USA. [Fetteresso g/s]

COLQUHOUN, JAMES, born 1804, son of Frederick Colquhoun and
Jane Hanson, died in Berlin, Canada, 11.9.1877.
[Edinburgh, St Cuthbert's, g/s]

COLQUHOUN, General LUDOVIC, born 1808, died in Texas 1878.
[Luss g/s]

COLQUHOUN, WILLIAM, born 1861, son of Allan Colquhoun
{1822-1904} and Jane Davidson {1826-1867}, died in Glenspey,
Sullivan County, New York, 23.2.1899. [Renfrew g/s]

COLTART, JAMES, born 1815, son of William Coltart and Marion
Good, died in Canada West 1.8.1887. [Balmaclellan g/s]

COLTART, MARY, born 1818, daughter of William Coltart and
Marion Good, died in Paris, Brantford township, Upper Canada,
15.8.1847. [Balmaclellan g/s]

COLTART, ROGER, born 1767, son of Robert Coltart and Janet Reid,
"late of Fredericksburg, Virginia", died 1803. [Buittle g/s]

COLTART, SETH, born 1809, son of James Coltart and Marion .....,
died in California 29.10.1851. [Buittle g/s]

COMRIE, WILLIAM JAMES, son of John Comrie and Euphemia
Fettes, died in Philadelphia 5.12.1887. [Laurencekirk g/s]

CONACHER, ALEXANDER, born 1846, son of David Conacher and
Helen Stewart, died in USA 10.9.1897. [Moulin g/s]

CONLEY, WILLIAM, born 1845, died in Carson City, Nevada,
9.1.1898. [Parton g/s]

COOPER, EDWIN, born 1868, died in USA 22.8.1858. [Anwoth g/s]

CORMACK, DONALD ANGUS, son of George Cormack and
Margaret Cormack, died in South Dakota 7.1901. [Anwoth g/s]

CORMACK, PETER, born 1880, son of James Cormack {1846-1909}
and Christina Anderson {1851-1924}, died in Detroit 13.7.1908.
[Clunie g/s]

CORRIE, WILLIAM, born 1873, died in Mobile, Alabama 4.6.1889.
[Borgue g/s]

COSSAR, HELEN, born 1840, daughter of David Cossar and Ann
Law, died in Memphis, USA, 20.9.1878. [Coldingham g/s]

COUGHTRIE, MARGARET, born 1825, daughter of Alexander
Coughtrie and Eleanor McWilliam, drowned in the wreck of the
Hungarian near Sable Island, Nova Scotia, 20.2.1860.
[Borgue g/s]

COUL, JOHN, born 1821, son of John Coul and Ann Bissett, died in
Windsor, California, 3.12.1878. [Leuchars g/s]

COUTTS, GEORGE D., born 1852, son of William Coutts {1827-
1898} a blacksmith at Anguston Quarry and Elspet F. Gregory
{1828-1863}, died in USA 22.4.1876. [Peterculter g/s]

COUTTS, WILLIAM, son of William Coutts {1785-1872} and Janet
Bain {1805-1888}, settled in St George, New Brunswick.
[Fettercairn g/s]

COWAN, ALEXANDER, born 1783, son of Thomas Cowan {1757-
1828} the Customs Controller of Bo'ness and Agnes Drummond
{1762-1799}, died in St John, New Brunswick, 29.6.1810.

[Bo'ness, Lower Wynd, g/s]

COWAN, ALEXANDER DOUGLAS, born 1849, son of David Cowan and Jane Douglas, died in New York 22.6.1895. [Dalry g/s]

COWAN, DAVID, born 1830, son of William Cowan {1807-1889} and Julia Sim {1799-1875}, a merchant in Toronto, died in Winnipeg 13.1.1882, buried in Mount Pleasant Cemetery, Toronto. [Rattray g/s]

COWAN, DAVID, born 1837, son of John Cowan and Janet Mill, died in St Francis, Canada, 3.11.1875. [Dunbarney g/s]

COWAN, ISABELLA, born 1853, daughter of David Cowan and Jane Douglas, died in New York 2.11.1892. [Dalry g/s]

COWAN, MARY, born 1837, daughter of William Cowan and Julia Sim, wife of John Hillock in Toronto, died 23.2.1896, buried at Mount Pleasant, Toronto. [Rattray g/s]

COWIE, WILLIAM, born 20.7.1809, son of James Cowie, merchant in Montrose, {1758-1837}, and Catherine Gairdner, {1768-1818}, died in Port Mississanga, Lake Huron, 28.4.1836. [Montrose g/s]

CRAIG, JAMES, born 1818, son of D. Craig and M. Mather, died 18.7.1860 in Pueblo County, Colorado Territory. [Eaglesham g/s]

CRAIG, JOHN, born 1788, son of Thomas Craig and Helen Young, died in Albany, New York, 11.1.1832. [Llanbryde g/s]

CRAIG, JOHN, born 1842, died in America 11.3.1886. [Colvend g/s]

CRAIG, ROBERT, born 1877, son of John Craig, died in America 7.4.1886. [Colvend g/s]

CRAIG, WILLIAM, born 1862, son of William Craig and Marjory Hay, died in Germantown, USA, 19.8.1909. [Arbirlot g/s]

CRAIGIE, SUSAN, relict of John Craigie in Quebec, died 8.1838. [Edinburgh, New Calton, g/s]

CRAIK, MARY, born 1797, died in Hallsco ..., Benbrook, Canada West. 11.2.1874. [Southwick g/s]

CRAWFORD, JAMES, born 1815, son of Hugh Crawford. {1782-1866}, farmer in Galston, and Euphemia White, {1788-1878}, died in Delaware 29.8.1848. [Loudoun g/s]

CRAWFORD, WILLIAM RONALD, born 11.3.1826, died at Clinton Furnace, Kenrucky, 1851. [Kirkoswald g/s]

CREE, JOHN MATTHEW, born 1880, son of Gavin Cree and Marion Russell, died in USA 1916. [Biggar g/s]

CREIGHTON, WILLIAM, born 1850, son of Alexander Creighton and Eliza McRobert, died on Clark's Island, Maine, 11.5.1895. [Dalbeattie g/s]

CRICHTON, JOHN, born 1801, son of John Crichton {1765-1826} a slater, and Margaret Purves, {1777-1807}, died in Brockville, Canada West, 16.4.1854. [Chirnside g/s]

CROLL, ANDREW, born 1821, son of Charles Croll and Janet Mitchell, died in Quebec 18.6.1848. [St Andrews g/s]

CROOKS, JANE, born 1810, daughter of James Crooks {1788-1854}, a merchant in Cockburnspath, and Agnes Crerar, {1785-1847}, died in St Lewis, USA, 26.6.1849. [Cockburnspath g/s]

CRUICKSHANK, A.A., born 1845, 'late of Boston, USA', died in Inverarity 4.12.1877. [Fern g/s]

CUMMING, JACOBINA, born 1833, daughter of John Cumming and Elizabeth Bell, wife of James Russell, died in Canada 28.1.1868. [Maybole g/s]

CUNNINGHAM, ALEXANDER, died in New York 29.5.1892. [Dunbar g/s]

CUNNINGHAM, JAMES, son of John Cunningham and Janet Ewing, died in Boston, Massachusetts, 19.11.1912. [Bonhill g/s]

CUNNINGHAM, JOHN, in New York 18... [Melrose g/s]

CUSHNY, THOMAS, born 31.3.1812, son of Arthur Cushny and Alison Minto, died in Natchez, Georgia, 10.1837. [Peebles g/s]

CUTHBERT, JAMES, of Berthier, Member of HM Legislative Council of Canada, son of David Cuthbert {1715-1781}. [Culross g/s]

CUTHBERT, JAMES, born 1867, son of Andrew Cuthbert and Jane Bell, died in Chicago 9.8.1896. [Kirkbuddo g/s]

CUTHBERT, JAMES, born 1869, died in Watertown, New York, 8.1.1911. [Caputh g/s]

CUTHBERT, WILLIAM, born in Ayrshire, a merchant in New Richmond, Bay of Chaleur, died in Cheshire 3.8.1854. [Greenock g/s]

CUTHBERTSON, MARGARET, born 1814, daughter of David Cuthbertson and Jane Rankin, died in Canada 12.4.1866. [Kilmaurs g/s]

DAISIE, MARGARET, daughter of John Daisie {1783-1834} and
Agnes Robertson {1790-1874}, wife of William Sturgeon, died in
Westerly, Rhode Island, 5.1849. [Anstruther Easter g/s]

DALGLEISH, CATHERINE CRAIG, daughter of Adam Dalgleish
{1794-1855} and Martha Cameron {1808-1858}, settled in San
Francisco. [Tulliallan g/s]

DALL, WILLIAM, born 1797, died in Racine, Wisconsin, 24.5.1877.
[Newburgh, Fife, g/s]

DALLING, MARY, born 1794, daughter of John Dalling in Boatcroft,
{1761-1831}, died in White Pigeon, USA, 10.1854.
[Balmaghie g/s]

DALZIEL, JANET, born 1821, daughter of William Dalziel and
Margaret Currie, died in Canada 23.9.1850. [Fenwick g/s]

DALZIEL, ROBERT, born 1824, son of William Dalziel and Margaret
Currie, died in Memphis 3.10.1864. [Fenwick g/s]

DANIEL, ROBERT, born 1814, son of Thomas Damiel and Alice
Nash, a merchant in Baltimore around 1840, died in England
17.6.1873. [Dumfries g/s]

DARLING, ALEXANDER BARCLAY, born 1852, son of William
Darling a merchant and Elizabeth Anderson, a minister in
Waskada, Manitoba, died 15.8.1903. [Dunbar g/s]

DARLING, GEORGE BENNET, born 1849, son of David Darling,
died in Chicago 22.5.1880. [Chirnside g/s]

DAVIDSON, ALEXANDER, born 1800, son of Thomas Davidson
{1758-1846}, died in Savannah 25.12.1825.
[Kilbride, Arran, g/s]

DAVIDSON, DAVID, born 1840, son of Thomas Davidson and Agnes
Valentine, died in USA 4.9.1887. [Glamis g/s]

DAVIDSON, GEORGE, born 1814, son of John Davidson {1777-
1853} a merchant in Aberdeen, and his wife Margaret {1779-
1866}, Sheriff of Waterloo County, Canada, died 27.4.1881.
[Dyce g/s]

DAVIDSON, JAMES W., born 1820, died in Newfoundland
14.4.1837. [Anwoth g/s]

DAVIDSON, JAMES V., born 17.6.1820, son of Thomas Davidson
and Agnes Valentine, died in USA 26.12.1866. [Glamis g/s]

DAVIDSON, JAMES, born 1843, late of Overtown, Dyce, died in
Carman, Manitoba, 13.3.1908. [Dyce g/s]

DAVIDSON, LACHLAN, son of Samuel Davidson {1747-1817} and Isabella Grant {1748-1817}, settled in Canada West. [Alvie g/s]

DAVIDSON, MARGARET, born 1818, daughter of John Davidson {1777-1853} a merchant in Aberdeen, and his wife Margaret {1779-1853}, wife of William Fisher, died in Toronto 3.4.1885. [Dyce g/s]

DAVIDSON, MARGERY, born 17.3.1829, daughter of Thomas Davidson and Agnes Valentine, died in USA 11.6.1885. [Glamis g/s]

DAVIDSON, ROBERT T., born 1793, died in Texas 30.6.1838. [Anwoth g/s]

DAVIDSON, ROBERT T., born 1820, died on the Banks of Newfoundland 14.4.1837. [Anwoth g/s]

DAVIDSON, ..., son of ... Davidson {died 1757} a farmer in Pityoulish, and Mary Grant {died 179.}, a merchant in Washington, D.C. [Kincardine Strathspey g/s]

DENHOLM, GEORGE, born 1813, died in Montreal 24.8.1891. [Coulter g/s]

DENNISON, JAMES, born 1755 in Culreach, schoolmaster of Balmaghie, then in Virginia, died in Gatehouse 19.12.1824. [Anwoth g/s]

DENNISON, ROBERT SCARTH, son of James Dennison {1806-1875} and Margaret Wallace {1798-1874}, settled in Winsted, Connecticut. [St Magnus, Stronsay, g/s]

DENNISTON, ROBERT, born 7.8.1816, died in Toronto 7.3.1853. [Whithorn Old g/s]

DEUCHAR, ROBERT, only son of Robert Deuchar and Margaret Ritchie, died in Cincinatti 10.4.1863. [Edinburgh, Greyfriars, g/s]

DEWAR, MARY, born 20.5.1810, daughter of Dr Henry Dewar of Lassodie, married Gilman Kimball MD, died in Lowell, Massachusetts, 7.7.1869. [Dumfries g/s] [Edinburgh, St Cuthbert's, g/s]

DEWAR, PETER, born 1812, son of Donald Dewar in Qupig, {1760-1826} and Helen Murray {1776-1839}, died in America 2.1837. [Moonzievaird g/s]

DICK, JAMES, born 16.1.1743, son of Alexander Dick and Janet Martin, died in South Carolina 6.1770. [Dalry g/s]

DICK, JAMES, born 1777, son of John Dick {1747-1833} and Janet
Dick {1742-1828}, died in Canada 6.1821.
[Bathgate Kirkton g/s]

DICK, WILLIAM, born 1799, son of William Dick {1765-1816} a
machinemaker in Dundee, and Euphemia Drummond {1771-
1835}, died in Montgomery, Alabama, 1.1832.
[Dundee, Howff, g/s]

DICK, WILLIAM, born 1868, son of William Dick and Christina
Robb, died in Ansonia, Connecticut, 27.10.1889.
[Longforgan g/s]

DICKSON, DAVID, born 1811, son of Reverend David Dickson, died
in Valparaiso, USA, 10.4.1884. [Edinburgh, St Cuthbert's, g/s]

DICKSON, MARGARET, born 1827, daughter of Alexander Dickson
and Jane Henry, wife of Robert Johnstone, died in New York
5.5.1851. [Anwoth g/s]

DICKSON, MARY, daughter of George Dickson and Agnes ...., died
in Dallas, Texas, 30.9.1887, buried in Trinity Cemetery, Dallas.
[Coldingham g/s]

DOBIE, DAVID, born 1809, son of William Dobie and Mary Lindsay,
died in Quebec 14.7.1831. [Southwick g/s]

DOLLAR, JAMES, born 6.1849 in Grahamston, son of William Dollar
and Mary Melville, died in San Rafael. California, 3.1898.
[Falkirk g/s]

DOLLAR, WILLIAM, died in Ottawa 1873, buried in Beechwood
Cemetery. [Falkirk g/s]

DON, WILLIAM, born 1792, son of Alexander Don and Janet
Prophet, died in Montreal 1.1850. [Strathcathro g/s]

DON, WILLIAM CARNEGIE, born 1853, son of James Don and
Mary Carnegie, died 1877, buried in Quincy, Iowa.
[Brechin Cathedral g/s]

DONALD, ALEXANDER, born 1882, son of Lewis Donald {1829-
1904} a farmer, died in Winnipeg 23.12.1910. [Echt g/s]

DONALD, Mrs ANN, died in New Orleans 1.5.1858.
[Dundee, Howff, g/s]

DONNAN, JOHN, born 1810, son of John Donnan, {1766-1829},
tenant in Culscadden, died in Pittsburgh 28.6.1838.
[Whithorn Old g/s]

DOUGALL, ROBERT KIRKLAND, born 1863, son of William
Dougall and Mary Kirkland, died in Timberline, Cabaline,
Montana, 21.9.1890. [Cambusnethan g/s]

DOUGHTIE, WILLIAM, A.R.C.A., born 1848, son of William
Doughtie {1811-1851} and Isabella Dall {1808-1881}, died in
Orlando, USA, 1883. [Edinburgh, New Calton, g/s]

DOUGLAS, DAVID, born in Scone 1798, botanist, died in the
Sandwich Islands 1834. [New Scone g/s]

DOUGLAS, JAMES SWORD, son of George Douglas and Jane
Moore, died in Canada 1835. [Rothesay g/s]

DOUGLAS, JOHN, born 1840, son of William Douglas, messenger-at-
arms in Perth, and Jane ..., died in Stratford, Ontario, 4.5.1864.
[Perth, Greyfriars, g/s]

DOUGLAS, JOHN, born 1830, son of Archibald Douglas and Helen
Bain, died in California 18.3.1889. [Sannox g/s]

DOUGLAS, Dr ROBERT, born 1814, son of William Douglas {1785-
1853} and Janet Walker {1788-1868}, a physician in New York,
died in New York 25.7.1861. [Johnstone g/s]

DOUGLAS, ROBERT, born 1794, late Captain of the Royal Canadian
Rifles, died in Bowmore, Islay, 9.9.1869. [Bowmore g/s]

DOUGLAS, WILLIAM, born 1798, died in Montreal 11.3.1833.
[Monigaff g/s]

DOW, GEORGE, born 1861, son of Alexander Dow and Margaret
Donaldson, died in Edmonton, Canada, 1912. [Methven g/s]

DOW, WILLIAM, son of Dr William Dow {1765-1844} and Anne
Mason, settled in Montreal. [Muthill g/s]

DOWNIE, GEORGE HART, born 1828, son of John M. Downie
{1806-1867} and Marion Hart {1801-1866}, died in Lefroy,
Ontario, 16.5.1867. [Edinburgh, Grange, g/s]

DOWNS, ALEXANDER, born 1822, died in Canton, Massachusetts,
18.1.1865. [South Leith g/s]

DRUMMOND, JOHN, born 1843, son of William Drummond, died in
New York 11.11.1902. [Strageath g/s]

DRYSDALE, ALEXANDER ADOLPHUS EDWARD, born in Canada
21.3.1852, son of Alexander and Janet Drysdale, died in Pau,
Pyrenees, France, 20.3.1879. [Dunbar g/s]

DRYSDALE, STELLA, born in Canada 28.5.1850, son of Alexander
and Janet Drysdale, died in Dunbar 28.6.1868. [Dunbar g/s]

DUFF, HARRIET REID, daughter of John Duff {1803-1890}, settled in Montreal. [Cargill g/s]

DUFF, WILLIAM L., Lieutenant Colonel of the 2nd Illinois Regiment of Artillery, died in the US Civil War 1861-1865. [Old Calton g/s]

DUGUID, WILLIAM, born 1754, youngest son of John Duguid and Helen Johnston, sometime a merchant in Baltimore, North America, died in Granite Place, Aberdeen, 18.8.1821. [Udny g/s]

DUNCAN, ALEXANDER, born 25.5.1805, settled in Providence, USA, died in Knossington 14.10.1889. [Craig Inchbrioch g/s]

DUNCAN, DONALD, son of James Duncan {died 1823}, a merchant in Greenock, and Elizabeth Shaw {died 1806}, settled in St Louis, Missouri. [Greenock, Inverkip St., g/s]

DUNCAN, JAMES, born 1772, son of William Duncan and Agnes Sime, died in Savannah, America, 1798. [Kilmany g/s]

DUNCAN, JAMES, born 1869, son of James Duncan {1828-1892} a farmer in Muirton, died in Dawson City, Klondyke, 24.7.1899. [Belhelvie g/s]

DUNCAN, JOHN, son of John Duncan {1736-1786} a wright in Perth, and Ann Simpson {1747-1829}, died in Charleston, South Carolina. [Perth, Greyfriars, g/s]

DUNCANSON, ALEXANDER, son of Alexander Duncanson {1768-1839} and Jean Cumming {1778-1848}, died in Charleston, South Carolina, 14.9.1838. [Ramshorn, Glasgow, g/s]

DUNDAS, ELIZABETH, born 1817, died in Boston 12.3.1892. [Edzell g/s]

DUNDAS, JAMES, born 1842, settled in Boston, died in New York 16.1.1890. [Edzell g/s]

DUNDAS, WILLIAM, born 1816, son of William Dundas and Isabel Smith, died in Boston 12.3.1892. [Edzell g/s]

DUNLOP, ALEXANDER, born 1851, son of Alexander Dunlop {1812-1879} and Janet Dickson {1818-1858}, died in Holstein, Ontario, 27.8.1880. [Bathgate, Kirkton, g/s]

DUNLOP, WILLIAM, son of Alexander Dunlop, educated in Glasgow University, ordained as a minister 1679, settled in Carolina, died in Glasgow 3.1700. [Glasgow University g/s]

DUNLOP, WILLIAM B., born 1847, son of James Usher Dunlop a
merchant in Leith and Annie Thomson, died in Chicago
1.10.1880. [Edinburgh, Greyfriars, g/s]

DUNN, JAMES, born 1841, son of Peter Dunn and Jane Ritchie, died
in San Francisco, California, 13.8.1929. [Greenock g/s]

DUNN, JOHN RITCHIE, born 1844, son of Peter Dunn and Jane
Ritchie, died in San Francisco, California, 1.11.1880.
[Greenock g/s]

DUNNET, GEORGE, born 1845, son of James Dunnet and Barbara
Brotchie, died in Boston, Massachusetts, 7.5.1891. [Dunnet g/s]

DURIE, ADAM, born 1857, son of John Durie and Jane Edward, died
on Deals Island, Maryland, 5.9.1875. [Montrose, Rosehill, g/s]

DYER, ALEXANDER, jr., born 1850, son of Alexander Dyer, a tea
merchant and Janet Robertson, died 27.8.1874, buried in Mount
Royal Cemetery, Montreal. [Canongate g/s]

EDDINGTON, JAMES GILLESPIE, born 1837, son of George
Eddington and Grace Gillespie, died in Woodstock, Canada,
14.3.1890. [Carnwath g/s]

EDWARD, GEORGE, born 1847, died in America 1873.
[Bathgate, Boghead, g/s]

EDWARDS, JAMES, born 1861, son of Alexander Edwards {1831-
1901} and Ann Mackie {1831-1895}, died in Delmont, USA,
2.10.1893. [Broughty Ferry, St Aidan's, g/s]

EDWARDS, JOHN, born 1779, son of James Edwards and Elspet
Bannerman, died in Clarence, Canada West, 4.1842.
[Kinnedar, Moray, g/s]

ELLIOT, WILLIAM, son of John Elliot {1787-1863} tenant in
Chesterhall and Susan Davidson {1798-1869}, died in New York
aged 61. [Melrose g/s]

ELLIS, DAVID, born 1821, son of Fletcher Ellis and Madeline
Davidson, a ships carpenter, died in St John's, Newfoundland,
7.1851. [Arbroath Abbey g/s]

ERVING, ANN, born 1741, daughter of John Erving, late of Boston,
Massachusetts, widow of Duncan Stewart of Ardshiel, died in
Edinburgh 13.12.1804. [St Cuthbert's, Edinburgh, g/s]

EWART, ROBERT BRUNTON, born 1809, son of Robert Ewart and
Charlotte Ritchie, died in Stratford, Canada West, 13.4.1852.
[Edinburgh, St Cuthbert's, g/s]

EWING, DUNCAN M., son of ... Ewing and Janet Barr {1770-1809}, settled in New York. [Houston g/s]

EWING, ELLEN, born 1832, daughter of James Ewing, wife of James Christie, died in Hastings, Canada, 10.5.1887. [Galston g/s]

EWING, JANE WILSON, born 1807, died in Toronto 10.4.1884. [Galston g/s]

EWING, JOHN, born 1835, son of William Leckie Ewing and Eleanor McFarlan, died in Manitoba 1895. [Kippen g/s]

EWING, PETER, born in Paisley 1803, a merchant in Montreal, died in Paisley 5.11.1845. [Paisley Woodside g/s]

EWING, ROBERT, born 1828, died in Buffalo, USA, 24.11.1893. [Galston g/s]

EWING, WILLIAM, born 1785 in the Vale of Leven, educated at Glasgow University, '50 years resident in the southern states of USA and tutor of eminent statesmen of Virginia', died in Glasgow 27.4.1865. [Bonhill g/s]

EWING, WILLIAM, died 15.4.1901, buried in Montreal. [Stirling g/s]

FAIRWEATHER, JOHN, born 1829, son of John Fairweather and Ann Milne, died in Plymouth, Massachusetts, 2.4.1855. [Montrose, Rosehill, g/s]

FALCONER, PATRICK, born 1775, son of William Falconer {1720-1793} a farmer, and Anna Rose {1743-1821}, a merchant, died in New York 1837. [Inveraven g/s]

FALCONER, ROBERT, born 1782, son of William Falconer {1720-1793} a farmer, and Anna Rose {1743-1821}, a merchant, died in New York 1851. [Inveraven g/s]

FALCONER, WILLIAM, born 1736, former Governor of Severn Fort, Hudson Bay, later feuar in Garmouth, died 1.12.1801, husband of Ann Morrison {1754-1840}. [Essil g/s]

FARQUHAR, ALEXANDER, born 1834, son of Robert Farquahar and Margaret Proctor, died in Omaha, USA, 7.5.1873. [Llanbryde g/s]

FARQUHARSON, CHARLES, born 1779, son of James Farquharson and Ann Stuart, sometime in Ballitrian, Kirkmichael, died in Baltimore, Maryland, 2.6.1860. [Inveraven Downan g/s]

FARQUHARSON, MARGARET, born 1779, wife of John Callam, died in Canada 8.1870. [Glenbuchat g/s]

FARQUHARSON, ROBERT, born 1777, son of James Farquharson and Anne Stuart sometime in Ballitruan, Kirkmichael, died in Nashville, Tennessee, 28.6.1856. [Inveraven Downan g/s]

FARQUHARSON, ROBERT ALEXANDER, born 1845, son of Donald Farquharson a postman in Ballater, died in Fort San Juan, Washington Territory, USA, 29.12.1875. [Glencairn g/s]

FARQUHARSON, WILLIAM, born 1803, son of William Farquharson and Christine Logan, died at Branch Hill, Alexandria on the Red River, USA, 13.8.1848. [Montrose g/s]

FAULDS, JAMES, son of George Faulds {1820-1885} and Anne Smith {1823-1914}, died in Dawson City, Canada, 1911. [Lennoxtown g/s]

FEA, ISABELLA J.Y., born 1874, wife of J.M.Yorston, died 20.10.1898, buried in Lilloet Cemetery, British Columbia. [Lady g/s, Stronsay][St Magnus, Kirkwall, g/s]

FELL, MARGARET RATTRAY, born 1841, daughter of James Fell {1811-1889} and Margaret Gow {1813-1885}, died in Kansas City 27.10.1880. [Kinloch g/s]

FERGUSON, DAVID, born 28.2.1820, son of James Ferguson {1794-1878} and Mary Alexander {1795-1877}, died 5.4.1859, buried at Point St Charles, Montreal. [Bathgate, Boghead, g/s]

FERGUSON, DOUGALD, born 1773, master of the brig Fair Lady, drowned off the Banks of Newfoundland 5.1.1829. [Greenock g/s]

FERGUSON, DUNCAN, born 1785, son of John Ferguson and Margaret McDougall, died in Ross, Canada, 20.10.1853. [Comrie, Tullichetttle, g/s]

FERGUSON, GEORGE, born 1844, son of James Ferguson and Elizabeth Valentine, died in Brooklyn, USA, 16.7.1869. [Liff g/s]

FERGUSON, JAMES, son of Joseph Ferguson and Nichola Hair, died in Toronto 1.7.1836. [Dumfries g/s]

FERGUSON, JAMES, born 1836, son of James Ferguson {died 1853} and Mary Harvey {died 1848}, died in San Antonio, Texas, 1866. [Stirling, Holy Rude, g/s]

FERGUSON, JANET, born 1855, daughter of William Ferguson and Janet McKenzie, died in Pawtucket, USA, 27.3.1889. [Coupar Angus g/s]

FERGUSON, JOHN, son of James Ferguson {died 1853} and Mary
    Harvey {died 1848}, settled in London, Canada.
    [Stirling, Holy Rude, g/s]
FERGUSON, ROBERT, soldier of F Company, 97th Regiment of New
    York Infantry Volunteers, died in the US Civil War 1861-1865.
    [Edinburgh, Old Calton, g/s]
FERGUSON, WILLIAM, born 1849, son of Alexander Ferguson and
    Agnes Brown, died in Philadelphia 23.3.1886. [Stewarton g/s]
FERRIER, JAMES, son of George Ferrier {1771-1814} and Elizabeth
    Bayne {1767-1834}, settled in Montreal before 1841.
    [Auchtermuchty g/s]
FETTES, AGNES, born 1833, daughter of William Fettes and Harriet
    Donaldson, died in America 21.2.1860. [Dunnichen g/s]
FINDLAY, ANN, daughter of George Findlay {1788-1849} and Anne
    ...., died in Kingston, Upper Canada, 1843. [Cullen g/s]
FINDLAY, DAVID, born 28.11.1860, son of Captain Andrew Findlay
    and Jessie Baxter, died in Junction City, Kansas, 16.11.1886.
    [Craig Inchbrioch g/s]
FINDLAY, JESSIE, born 11.6.1858, daughter of Captain Andrew
    Findlay and Jessie Baxter, died in Junction City, Kansas,
    10.12.1888. [Craig Inchbroich g/s]
FINDLAY, THOMAS, born 1813, son of James Findlay {1780-1852}
    and Barbara Marshall {1794-1868}, died in New Orleans 1840.
    [St Clement's, Aberdeen, g/s]
FINDLAY, WILLIAM LYON, born 1861, son of Joseph Findlay
    {1810-1863} and Elisa Lyon {1827-1895}, died in Texas
    25.7.1879. [Johnstone g/s]
FINNIE, JAMES, son of Thomas Finnie, feuar in Greenock {died
    1838} and Janet Wilson {died 1882}, died 1863 in San Andreas,
    California. [Gourock, Chapel Street, g/s]
FISHER, ALEXANDER, born 1850, son of Alexander Fisher and Jane
    Alison Conacher, died in Ottawa 19.1.1912. [Little Dunkeld g/s]
FISHER, Dr JAMES, born 1756, late garrison surgeon in Montreal,
    died in Dunkeld 26.6.1822. [Dunkeld Cathedral g/s]
FLEMING, DAVID, born 1803, son of David Fleming {1758-1803} a
    dyer in Dundee, and Ann Nicoll {1767-1853}, died in Miramachi
    17.5.1821. [Dundee, Logie, g/s]

FLEMING, JOHN, born 1869, son of John Fleming {1832-1908} and
Jane ... {1828-1906}, died in Pittsburgh, USA, 10.1.1900.
[Bathgate, Kirkton, g/s]

FLEMING, T.S., born 1816, died in Nashville, USA, 15.6.1849.
[Buittle g/s]

FORBES, ALEXANDER, son of Duncan Forbes {1783-1839} a
blacksmith and Isabella Johnston {1792-1874}, a merchant in San
Francisco. [Old High Church, Inverness, g/s]

FORBES, ALEXANDER, born 1793, son of Arthur Forbes {1753-
1831}, Major of the 79th Highlanders, died in Kingston, Upper
Canada, 30.3.1851. [Stirling g/s]

FORBES, ARTHUR, born 1753, late of the North Carolina
Highlanders, died in Stirling 23.4.1831. [Stirling g/s]

FORBES, CHARLES, Captain of the 60th Regiment of Foot, died at
Ticonderoga 1758. [Banff g/s]

FORBES, GEORGE, born 1827, son of Reverend William Forbes and
Charlotte Mackay, died in Pamfton Plains, New Jersey,
15.4.1891. [Congarff g/s]

FORBES, JOHN, born 1864, son of James Forbes {1824-1865}, died
in Delaware 1903. [St Clement's, Aberdeen, g/s]

FORBES, ROBERT, born 1855, son of William Forbes and Margaret
Hopkins, died in Leadville, Colorado, 10.12.1891.
[St Andrews g/s]

FORBES, SOPHIA HORN, daughter of Alexander Forbes, wife of
James Grant, died in Montreal 20.11.1858.
[Edinburgh, St Cuthbert's, g/s]

FORREST, JAMES, born 1796, died in New York 24.1.1867.
[Bathgate, Kirkton, g/s]

FORREST, MARY, born 1839, daughter of Robert Forrest, died in
New Orleans 1853. [Carluke g/s]

FORSYTH, GEORGE, born 1827, son of John Forsyth and Marion
Hardie, died in Sinniconeck, Lewis County, Kentucky, 2.9.1854.
[Cockburnspath g/s]

FORSYTH, WILLIAM, born 1749, a merchant in Greenock and in
Nova Scotia, died 14.10.1814. [Tealing g/s]

FOULIS, PETER, born 1836, son of Robert Foulis, an engineer of the
Royal Navy, died in Bermuda 31.10.1875. [Aberdour g/s]

FOYER, ARCHIBALD EDMONSTON, born 1861, son of David
Foyer and Christina Muir, died in Sumner, Nebraska, .2.1907.
[Campsie g/s]

FOYER, DAVID MUIR, born 1862, son of Archibald Foyer, a grazier
in Knowhead, died in Sutherland, Nebraska, 8.12.1914.
[Campsie g/s]

FOYER, WILLIAM, born 1869, son of David Foyer and Christina
Muir, died in Sutherland, Nebraska, 10.9.1895. [Campsie g/s]

FRANCE, ROBERT, born 1827, son of Richard France and Isabella
Wilson, died at Fenelon Falls, Canada West, 25.2.1862.
[Cockburnspath g/s]

FRANK, WILLIAM BOUGH, born 1735, son of James Frank of
Boughbridge, Colonel and Collector of New York, died 1810.
[Eccles g/s]

FRASER, ANDREW, born 1882, son of Francis Fraser and Janet
Munro, died in Antelope, Oregon, 21.4.1909.
[Suddie, Black Isle, g/s]

FRASER, ANDREW, son of James Fraser {died 1846} and Catherine
Fraser {died 1846}, settled in Embo, Canada, by 1887.
[Glenconvinth g/s]

FRASER, ANGUS, born 1872, son of George Fraser and Helen
Urquhart, died in Manitoba 1.10.1914. [Clyne g/s]

FRASER, DONALD, son of John Fraser {1753-1838} and Isabel Clark
{1757-1796}, a merchant in Quebec. [Old Petty g/s]

FRASER, JANE, born 1820, daughter of John Fraser and Marjory
Roy, died in Lanark, Canada West, 8.1.1853. [Kilbarchan g/s]

FRASER, JOHN, son of John Ogg Fraser tenant in Ballindalloch of
Farraline and Janet Fraser {1745-1812}, a merchant in Halifax,
Nova Scotia. [Boleskine g/s]

FRASER, JOHN, born 1829, son of John Fraser {1789-1874} and
Marjory Roy {1794-1869}, died in Baltimore, USA, 2.9.1879.
[Kilbarchan East g/s]

FRASER, JOHN, born 1846, son of John Fraser and Ann Ferguson,
died in Ontario 2.10.1869. [Moulin g/s]

FRASER, JOHN FERGUSON, born 1839, son of John Fraser {1809-
1878} and Jane McGregor {1809-1865}, died in Kansas City
9.11.1922. [Greenock g/s]

FRASER, MARGARET, born 1826, daughter of John Fraser and
Marjory Roy, wife of Major C.E.Lindsay, United States Marine
Corps, died in Washington, D.C., 2.2.1886. [Kilbarchan g/s]

FRASER, PETER, born in Dingwall 17.2.1834, son of John Fraser
{1809-1878} and Jane McGregor {1809-1865}, died in San
Francisco 11.5.1862. [Greenock g/s]

FRASER, ROBERT, born 1869, son of John Fraser and Anne
Ferguson, died in Chicago 8.3.1909. [Moulin g/s]

FRASER, SIMON, settled in Montreal by 1822. [Boleskine g/s]

FRENCH, THOMAS, born 10.4.1830, son of John French and Jane
Herbert, died in Canada 20.6.1858. [Carnwath g/s]

FYFE, DAVID, born 1841, son of William Fyfe and Jane Young, died
in New York 19.8.1872, buried in New York Bay Cemetery.
[Friockheim g/s]

FYFE, JAMES, son of John P. Fyfe {1806-1865} and Ann Duncan
{1805-1877}, died at the Pier of Pennsylvania, America.
[Brechin Cathedral g/s]

FYFE, WILLIAM, born 1817, son of William Fyfe, {1785-1868}
Captain of the 92nd Regiment, and Barbara Burgess {1795-
1846}, died in New York 1.1850. [Essil g/s]

GALLOWAY, JOHN, born 1815, a baker, 'late of New York', died
31.1.1852. [Buchlyvie g/s]

GARDINER, JAMES, born 1832, son of Captain John Gardiner of
Carse Grange, a merchant in Abingdon, USA, died 15.9.1868.
[Errol g/s]

GARDNER, ARCHIBALD, born 11.3.1836, son of Archibald Gardner
of Nethercommon and Elizabeth Wylde, died in Montreal
25.7.1875. [Paisley, Woodside, g/s]

GARDNER, GEORGE, born 1833, son of George Gardner {1804-
1844}, died in America 4.1.1858. [Whithorn g/s]

GARDNER, JAMES, son of Matthew Gardner {died 1874} and
Euphemia Dalzell {died 1846}, settled in Allecan County,
Michigan. [Cambusnethan g/s]

GEDDES, JOHN, son of Alexander Geddes {1777-1859} and Elizabeth
Gregory {1784-1838}, died in America aged 20.
[Perth, Greyfriars, g/s]

GEMLO, JAMES EBENEZER, born 1853, son of John Gemlo and Mary Ann Grant, master of the barque Nina, died in the River St Lawrence, Canada, 20.10.1880, buried in Quebec.
[Montrose, Rosehill, g/s]

GEMMELL, JOHN, born 1818, son of John Gemmell and Helen Symington, died in Tuckersmith, Canada West, 12.7.1864.
[Anwoth g/s]

GIBB, CHARLES LYALL, born 12.9.1857, son of David Gibb and Helen Valentine, died in Seattle, USA, 15.11.1904.
[Abernethy, Perth, g/s]

GIBB, JAMES, son of John Gibb {1761-1802} farmer in Hillhead, and Jean Lawson {1756-1839}, settled in Montreal or Quebec before 1826. [Carluke g/s]

GIBB, JOHN, son of John Gibb {1761-1802} farmer in Hillhead, and Jean Lawson {1756-1839}, settled in Montreal or Quebec before 1826. [Carluke g/s]

GIBB, JOHN, son of John Gibb and Margaret Hardie, died in Pittsburgh, Pennsylvania, 1849.
[Bo'ness, Upper Church Wynd, g/s]

GIBB, ROBERT, son of John Gibb and Margaret Hardie, died in Pittsburgh, Pennsylvania, 6.4.1851.
[Bo'ness, Upper Church Wynd, g/s]

GIBB, THOMAS, son of John Gibb {1761-1802} farmer in Hillhead, and Jean Lawson {1756-1839}, settled in Montreal or Quebec before 1826. [Carluke g/s]

GIBBON, JOHN, son of George Gibbon {1734-1811} and Elizabeth Bowat, died in Detroit. [Kildrummy g/s]

GIBSON, DAVID DRUMMOND, born 26.12.1874, son of Archibald Gibson, died in Milwaukee, USA, 15.2.1916. [Crieff g/s]

GIBSON, ELIZABETH, born 1815, wife of Andrew Stiven, died in Goderich, Ontario, 11.5.1876. [Arbroath Abbey g/s]

GIBSON, ELLEN, born 1884, daughter of Archibald Gibson, died in Albany, USA, 15.5.1928. [Crieff g/s]

GIBSON, HUGH, son of Hugh C. Gibson and Mary Anne Denovan, died in Detroit 31.5.1898. [South Leith g/s]

GIBSON, JAMES, born 1727, son of Reverend Luke Gibson, a merchant in Virginia, died 1786. [Colvend g/s]

GIBSON, JOHN, son of William Gibson {1757-1835} and Janet
Henderson {1763-1829}, settled in America. [Colinton g/s]

GIBSON, MARGARET, born 1811, daughter of Walter Gibson and
Janet Riddick, died in North America 8.7.1847. [Southwick g/s]

GIBSON, PETER, son of William Gibson {1757-1835} and Janet
Henderson {1763-1829}, settled in America. [Colinton g/s]

GIBSON, ROBERT, born 1808, died in Pine Rock, USA, 2.7.1887.
[Buittle g/s]

GIBSON, WILLIAM, born 1810, son of William Gibson {1780-1868}
and Agnes Henry {1780-1858}, died in Illinois 12.8.1828.
[Buittle g/s]

GIBSON, WILLIAM, born 1827, son of Alexander Gibson and Jean
Mill, died in Toronto 25.12.1858. [Arbroath Abbey g/s]

GILCHRIST, ALEXANDER, born 1818, son of James Gilchrist and
Isabella Smith, died in St John, New Brunswick, 21.11.1867.
[Carluke g/s]

GILCHRIST, ANDREW, son of William Gilchrist {1755-1837} and
Janet Cameron {1760-1815}, died in Pacific Grove, California.
[Newmilns g/s]

GILCHRIST, GEORGE, born 1854, son of William Gilchrist and
Annie Polson, died in Indiana 30.9.1896. [Loth g/s]

GILCHRIST, MARGARET FORREST, born 1815, daughter of James
Gilchrist and Isabella Smith, died in St John, New Brunswick,
28.8.1848. [Carluke g/s]

GILCHRIST, THOMAS, born 1813, son of James Gilchrist and
Isabella Smith, a merchant in St John, New Brunswick, died
17.12.1856. [Carluke g/s]

GILES, ANNE MOIR, born in New Orleans 11.3.1838, daughter of
James Park Giles {1784-1848} and Anne Potter {1795-1867},
died in Edinburgh 18.5.1889. [Edinburgh, Greyfriars, g/s]

GILES, GRACE FRASER, born in Edinburgh 4.8.1836, daughter of
James Park Giles {1784-1848} and Ann Potter {1795-1867}, died
in New Orleans 11.9.1838. [Edinburgh, Greyfriars, g/s]

GILLANDERS, ALEXANDER, son of Lachland Gillanders {1769-
1844} a farmer in Kishorn, and Margaret Mackenzie {1773-
1832}, settled in Canada West. [Applecross/Kishorn g/s]

GILLESPIE, ALEXANDER, born 1819, son of George Gillespie and Helen Hamilton, a merchant in New York, died 21.4.1863. [Wiston g/s]

GILLESPIE, ELIZABETH AGNES, born 1827, daughter of Alexander Gillespie and Jane Menzies, died in Hamilton, Canada, 5.12.1890. [Wiston g/s]

GILLESPIE, GEORGE, born 1772, a merchant in Canada, died in Biggar 18.9.1842. [Wiston g/s]

GILLESPIE, GEORGE, born 1849, died in Victoria, British Columbia, 1921. [Wiston g/s]

GILLESPIE, ROBERT, born 1784, settled in Montreal, died in London 3.9.1863. [Wiston g/s]

GILLIES, DAVID MACDONALD, son of Donald Macdonald Gillies {1749-1845}, farmer in Achadh nan Loach, and Agnes McCallum {1776-1867}, died in London, Ontario, 1885. [Kilkerran, Argyll, g/s]

GILLIES, WILLIAM, born 1809, died in Manilla, Canada, 13.11.1868. [Kilkerran, Argyll, g/s]

GILMOUR, AGNES, born 1815, wife of James Hutchison {1808-1864}, died in Aldboro Township, Elgin County, Ontario, 9.12.1879. [Mearns, Renfrew, g/s]

GLASS, WILLIAM, son of James Glass {1765-1854} and Margaret MacGregor {died 1861}, died in Boston, USA, 1863. [Strathmartine g/s]

GLEN, JAMES, born 1870, died in Prince Albert, Sasketchewan, 8.1.1896. [Brechin Cathedral g/s]

GOLDIE, PETER, son of James Goldie and Helen Taylor, died 10.3.1859 in Milwaukee. [Campsie g/s]

GOLDIE, ROBERT, son of James Goldie and Helen Taylor, died in Sioux City 31.3.1876. [Campsie g/s]

GOOD, ANDREW, born 1778, son of Andrew Good {1740-1803} and Jean Laurie {1745-1817}, died in Danville, Kentucky, 3.11.1805. [Colinton g/s]

GORDON, DAVID, born 1793, son of Charles Gordon and Elizabeth Gibson, died in America 5.10.1819. [Aberlemno g/s]

GORDON, JAMES, born 16.1.1743, son of Sir Alexander Gordon of Earlston, died in South Carolina 1771. [Dalry g/s]

GORDON, JAMES, settled as a merchant in New York by 1846.
[Edinburgh, New Calton, g/s]

GORDON, JANE, born 1834, daughter of Samuel Gordon and Mary
Ramsay, wife of Hudson Cleator, died in Brantford, Canada,
26.11.1910. [Brechin Cathedral g/s]

GORDON, THOMAS, settled as a merchant in Three Rivers, Canada,
by 1846. [Edinburgh, New Calton, g/s]

GORRIE, DUNCAN, born 1773, died in Glengarry, North America,
by 1847. [Monzie g/s]

GORRIE, DUNCAN, born 1844, died at Gross Island on passage to
North America 1874. [Monzie g/s]

GORRIE, HELEN, born 1799, died in Glengarry, North America,
7.3.1868. [Monzie g/s]

GOURLEY, HUGH, born 1829, son of Robert Gourley and Elizabeth
Andison, died in New York 7.3.1872. [Musselburgh g/s]

GOURLAY, JOHN, born 1827, son of Robert Gourley and Elizabeth
Andison, died in Florida 29.8.1880. [Musselburgh g/s]

GOWANS, ANDREW, born 1836, son of James Gowans, mason in
Newton {1786-1852}, and Joan Wardlaw {1793-1869}, died in
America 1860. [Abercorn g/s]

GRAHAM, JAMES, born 1795, son of James Graham of Leuinsdale
{1769-1856} and Helen Steele {1766-1860}, died at Oak Creek,
Wisconsin, 28.9.1851. [Lesmahagow g/s]

GRAHAM, Reverend JAMES, died in Charleston, America, son of
Thomas Graham {1709-1769} a farmer in Seafield, and ....
{1712-1791}. [Livingstone g/s]

GRAHAM, JAMES, born 1840, son of John Graham and Mary Caird,
died in New York 25.2.1900. [Dalbeattie g/s]

GRANT, ANDREW, son of Duncan Grant in Ballintuim of Clachaig
{1771-1831} and Margaret Fraser {1777-1851}, settled at Rob
Roy Inn, Hamilton, Ontario. [Abernethy g/s]

GRANT, DAVID, born 1824, son of James Grant {1779-1855} a
farmer in Glenbeg, and Christina Dow {1795-1869}. died in
Canada 1860. [Inverallan g/s]

GRANT, ELIZABETH, daughter of Peter Grant {1760-1838} a
merchant in Grantown, and Isabella Ross {1785-1855}, died in
Canada 1859. [Inverallan g/s]

GRANT, JAMES, born 1783, son of James Grant {1747-1792} a
farmer, and Jean Fraser {1743-1820}, a wright in North
Carolina, died 1828. [Cromdale g/s]

GRANT, JOHN, son of Peter Grant {1760-1838} a merchant in
Grantown, and Isabella Ross {1785-1855}, died in Canada 1858.
[Inverallan g/s]

GRANT, JOHN, born 1864, son of John Grant, farmer in Daleigh, and
Annie Grant, died in Imperial, Nebraska, 14.6.1911. [Advie g/s]

GRANT, KENNETH, son of William Grant {died 1857} and Isabella
Ross {died 1841}, died in Galt, Canada, 1857. [Fodderty g/s]

GRANT, PETER, born 1824, died in New York 1.4.1888.
[Arbroath Abbey g/s]

GRANT, ROBERT, of Kincorth, born 3.3.1752, son of David Grant
and Margaret Grant, 'an original member of the North West
Company in Canada', died in Kincorth 10.8.1801.
[Cromdale g/s]

GRANT, WILLIAM, born 1828, son of James Grant, died in
Shreveport, America, 5.11.1853. [Lintrathen g/s]

GRANT, WILLIAM, born 1854, son of Hugh Grant and Annie Gunn,
died in New York 20.1.1928. [Golspie g/s]

GRANT, ..., daughter of Reverend John Grant and Janet Grant {1743-
1764}, settled in Pittsburg, Pennsylvania. [Rothes g/s]

GRASSICK, JOHN SAMUEL, born 1840, son of John Grassick, a
merchant in Toronto, died 11.8.1878. [Congarff g/s]

GRAY, JAMES, born 1855, son of Adam Gray and Barbara Veitch,
died in New York 9.6.1852. [Maybole g/s]

GRAY, JAMES, born 1827, son of James Gray {1798-1886} and
Margaret Taylor {1801-1881}, died in Philadelphia 1.11.1876.
[Bellie g/s]

GRAY, JAMES, born 1858, son of Andrew Gray and Annie Allan,
died in Bardonia, Rockland County, New York, 11.2.1915.
[Dundee, Eastern Necropolis, g/s]

GRAY, JANE, born 1830, daughter of John Gray and Janet Dodds,
wife of Robert Douglas, died in Canada West 26.7.1864.
[Coldstream g/s]

GRAY, WILLIAM, son of William Gray {1762-1827} and Elspeth
Wynd {1779-1854}, a builder in Philadelphia. [Longforgan g/s]

GREEN, GEORGE, born 1835, son of James Green {1823-1900} a
carpenter in Fochabers, and Susan Bremner {1804-1858}, died in
Bernardtown, Massachusetts, 1.7.1860. [Bellie g/s]

GREENHILL, DAVID, son of David Greenhill and Agnes Hill in
Russellmill, died in Hamilton, Canada West, 23.11.1873.
[Cupar g/s]

GREENHILL, JOHN, son of David Greenhill and Agnes Hill in
Russellmill, died in Hamilton, Canada West, 23.11.1873.
[Cupar g/s]

GREENHILL, JOHN, born 1811, son of David Greenhill and Agnes
Hill in Rusellmill, died in Binbrook, Canada West, 15.2.1868.
[Cupar g/s]

GREENHILL, PETER, son of James Greenhill and Ann Duncan, died
in St Louis 25.4.1875. [Abernethy, Perth, g/s]

GREENSHIELDS, JAMES, born 1877, son of Robert Greenshields,
died in Los Angeles, California, 6.4.1905. [Patna g/s]

GREIG, ROBERT, son of David Greig {1786-1859} and Anna ...
{1780-1848}, settled in Mobile, Alabama. [Kinghorn g/s]

GREIG, DAVID, born 1801 in Kilrenny, died in Greenland 10.8.1832.
[Boarhills g/s]

GREIG, DAVID, born 21.11.1810, son of Alexander Greig and Jane
Whittet, died in New York 10.9.1847.
[Edinburgh, St Cuthbert's, g/s]

GREIG, JOHN WHITTET, born 11.9.1813, son of Alexander Greig
and Jane Whittet, died in New Orleans 17.1.1848.
[Edinburgh, St Cuthbert's, g/s]

GREIG, ROBERT, son of David Greig {1786-1859} and Anna ....
{1786-1848}, settled in Mobile, Alabama. [Kinghorn g/s]

GRIERSON. GEORGE, born 1866, died in Manitoba 20.8.1891.
[Balmaclellan g/s]

GRIERSON, JOHN, born 1867, died in Dogs Pond Creek, Olds, North
West Territories, Canada, 17.6.1895. [Balmaclellan g/s]

GRIEVE, JAMES JAMIESON, son of James Grieve {1778-1848} a
builder and Barbara Jamieson {1778-1853}, died in Ashland,
Wisconsin, 20.7.1903. [North Berwick g/s]

GRIEVE, WILLIAM, born 1822, son of Walter Grieve {1787-1861}
tenant in Southfield and Christian Elliot {1786-1880}, died in
Keppel, Canada West, 4.8.1878. [Borthwick g/s]

GRUBB, JAMES, born 1815, a shipmaster, died in Philadelphia
21.5.1849. [Ferry Port on Craig g/s]

GUILD, DAVID, born 1795, a merchant, died in Philadelphia
5.3.1830. [Dundee, Howff, g/s]

GUNN, DONALD, born 4.1827, son of John Gunn and Margaret
Bruce, died in American Civil War. [Dirlot g/s]

GUNN, JAMES, born 1810, died in Prescott, Canada West, 16.1.1845.
[Wardlaw g/s]

GUNN, WILLIAM, born 1818, a merchant in Canada West, died in
Perth 7.12.1844. [Perth, Greyfriars, g/s]

HAINING, DAVID, born 1811, son of Thomas Haining, died in
Wisconsin 17.10.1847. [Borgue g/s]

HALDANE, JOHN, born 1775, son of George Haldane, late of the
Hudson Bay Company, died 11.10.1857. [Haddington g/s]

HALIBURTON, LACHLAN, born 1845, a stonecutter in Washington,
D.C., died in Dundee 21.11.1909. [Dundee, Western, g/s]

HALL, JOHN, born 1830, son of William Hall and Christina Purdie,
died in New York 29.6.1859. [Galashiels g/s]

HALL, JOHN, son of Robert Hall {1734-1816} and Margaret Barr
{1743-1821}, a shipmaster in Newfoundland. [Inchinnan g/s]

HAMILTON, ALEXANDER, born 1823, son of Alexander Hamilton,
died in Hamilton, Canada West, 9.11.1855. [Crosbie g/s]

HAMILTON, ALEXANDER, son of James Hamilton and Jessie
Beattie, died in Tenino, Washington, 26.8.1915. [Dalbeattie g/s]

HAMILTON, HUGH, born 1858, son of Hugh Hamilton and Mary
Craig, died in New York 26.7.1884. [Anwoth g/s]

HAMILTON, JESSIE, daughter of William Hamilton and Jean Peden,
died 15.2.1853, buried in Chicago. [Galston g/s]

HAMILTON, JOHN, born 1836, son of John Hamilton and Ann Galt,
died in America 3.9.1873. [Stewarton g/s]

HAMILTON, MARION, born 1825, daughter of James Hamilton and
Jean Watson, died in New York 2.6.1853. [Lesmahagow g/s]

HAMILTON, ROBERT, born 1784, died in Argyle, Lafayette County,
Wisconsin, 3.3.1859. [Carsphairn g/s]

HAMILTON, WILLIAM, born 1816, son of James Hamilton and
Martha Wallace, died in New York 9.1849.
[Kilmarnock, St Andrew's, g/s]

HAMILTON, WILLIAM, born 1836, son of William Hamilton and
Jean Peden, died 17.4.1867, buried in Chicago. [Galston g/s]

HAMILTON, WILLIAM, born in Dalhousie, Bay of Chaleurs,
Canada, 3.4.1845, son of William Hamilton, died in Greenock
13.3.1905. [Greenock g/s]

HAMILTON, WILLIAM, born 1858, son of John Hamilton and Ann
Muir, died in Toronto 24.10.1891. [Bonhill g/s]

HANNAH, AGNES, born 1844, daughter of George Hannah and Janet
Urie, died in America 30.9.1869. [Galston g/s]

HANNING, MARGARET, born 1840, wife of Hugh Wyllie, died in
East Douglas, Massachusetts, 7.8.1915. [Borgue g/s]

HARDIE, ADAM, born 1774, died in America 15.10.1859.
[Stichill g/s]

HARDIE, HENRY, born 1767, son of James Hardie {1720-1802}, a
merchant in Quebec, died 20.8.1805. [Gogar g/s]

HARDIE, ROBERT, born 1815, son of John Hardie and Elizabeth
Black, died in Canada 30.3.1877. [Benholm g/s]

HARDIE, WILLIAM, son of Alexander Hardie {1839-1889}, died in
Blackfoot, Idaho, 28.5.1912. [Rhynie g/s]

HARDY, WILLIAM FORRESTER, born 1.6.1833, died in Portland,
Maine, 26.4.1898. [Canongate g/s]

HARKIN, ALEXANDER, born in Melrose 1.5.1828, died in St Peters,
Minnesota, 16.9.1907. [Melrose g/s]

HARKIN, BARNEY, born 1819, died in USA 16.12.1897.
[Melrose g/s]

HARKIN, DAVID, son of Barney Harkin {died 1869} and Janet
Thompson {died 1840}, died in USA 21.5.1852. [Melrose g/s]

HARKNESS, THOMAS, born in L'Assumption, Lower Canada, 1800,
son of William Harkness and Elizabeth Corrie, died in London
13.8.1860. [Dumfries g/s]

HARKNESS, WALTER, born 1801, son of William Harkness and
Elizabeth Corrie, a surgeon, died in Canada 3.1.1834.
[Dumfries g/s]

HAWTHORNE, JOSEPH, born 1862, son of William Hawthorne and
Agnes McCulloch, died in Ladysmith, Vancouver, 3.10.1907,
buried at Great Falls Cemetery, Montana. [Whithorn g/s]

HAY, JAMES, born 1808, son of Alexander Hay and Jeannie Scott,
died in New Orleans 10.12.1835. [Kilconquhar g/s]

HAY, JEAN, born 1792, daughter of Alexander Hay, a brush manufacturer, died in Canada 1864. [Canongate g/s]

HAY, Reverend JOHN, died in Kincardine, Canada West, 13.7.1866. [Perth, Greyfriars, g/s]

HAY, JOHN, born 1817, son of Peter Hay {1786-1837} and Alison Bathgate {1795-1853}, died in Natchez 1844. [Edinburgh, New Calton, g/s]

HENDERSON, ANDREW, born 1794, late of Fisherbriggs, died in Montreal 23.9.1848. [Tyrie g/s]

HENDERSON, HENRY, son of Richard Henderson {1760-1815}, died in New York 5.2.1849. [Musselburgh g/s]

HENDERSON, JOHN, born 1831, son of William Henderson and Euphemia Gaskie, died in Missouri 22.2.1860. [Kilmarnock g/s]

HENDERSON, PETER, son of James Henderson {1781-1848} and Katherine Wyse, a merchant in St John, Newfoundland, died at Rosebank 18.4.1826.[Falkirk g/s]

HENDERSON, STEPHEN, settled in New Orleans by 1831, [Dunblane g/s]

HENDERSON, WALTER, born 3.1844, son of John Henderson, died in San Francisco 5.1884. [Edinburgh, St Cuthbert's, g/s]

HENDERSON, WILLIAM, son of James Henderson a contractor {died 1835}, died in Quebec 28.8.18.. aged 35. [Dalmeny g/s]

HENDRY, ALEXANDER ROBERT, born 1873, son of James Hendry, farmer, {1829-1891}, died in Halifax, Nova Scotia, 14.12.1900, buried at Camphill Cemetery there. [Belhelvie g/s]

HENRY, Captain ARCHIBALD, born 1793, son of Thomas Henry of Buraston {1756-1845} and Lillias Henry {1772-1820}, died on the River Mississippi 3.1837. [Walls g/s]

HENRY, MARGARET MARY, born in New Brunswick, USA, (sic), 9.2.1854, daughter of George Henry, died in Edinburgh 19.11.1857. [Edinburgh, St Cuthbert's, g/s]

HEUCHAN, ROBERT, born 1838, son of William Heuchan and Mary Carlyle, died at New River, America, 15.11.1873. [Kirkgunzeon g/s]

HEUGH, JOHN, born 1813, son of Walter Heugh {1776-1854} and Janet Bald {1787-1837}, died in Philadelphia 31.7.1857. [Airth g/s]

HEUGH, WALTER, born 1816, son of Walter Heugh {1776-1854} and
Janet Bald {1787-1837}, died in Jersey City, USA, 6.12.1876.
[Airth g/s]

HEUGH, WILLIAM, born 1811, son of Walter Heugh {1776-1854}
and Janet Bald {1787-1837}, died in Nevada City, USA,
21.8.1867. [Airth g/s]

HEUGHAN, CHARLES, born 1803, son of James Heughan and .....
Duff, died in St John's, New Brunswick, 19.1.1832. [Buittle g/s]

HEUGHAN, WILLIAM, died in New York 25.4.184- aged 36.
[Buittle g/s]

HILL, ESTHER DUCHE, relict of Reverend William Hill of New
York, daughter of Reverend Jacob Duche in Philadelphia, died
27.12.1835. [Edinburgh, New Calton, g/s]

HOGG, ALEXANDER, born 1767, son of John Hogg and Julia
McLean, a surgeon, died in Charleston, America, 1804.
[Fogo g/s]

HOGG, JOHN, son of James Hogg {1768-1833} and Annie Stewart,
died in New York aged 33. [Dumfries g/s]

HOGG, Captain JOSEPH, died in Quebec 13.6.1866. [Polmont g/s]

HONEYMAN, DAVID, born 1817, son of Charles Honeyman and
Agnes Philip, died in America 8.1849. [Monimail g/s]

HONYMAN, Dr ROBERT, son of Reverend James Honyman {1703-
1780} and Katherine Allardyce, a physician in Virginia.
[Kinneff g/s]

HOOD, MARGARET, died in Quebec 3.1.1861. [Dundee, Howff, g/s]

HOOD, MATTHEW, born 1844, son of James Hood and Margaret
Crawford, died in Detroit, Canada, (sic), 11.9.1874.
[Kilmarnock, St Andrews, g/s]

HOOD, ROBERT, a merchant in Missouri, husband of Jessie Bennet
Keiller {1802-1843}. [Dundee, Howff, g/s]

HORN, JEAN, born 1851, daughter of .... Horn and Jean Shearer,
widow of William McAlister in Pittsburgh, died in Pittsburgh
2.11.1912. [Baldernock g/s]

HORNE, JESSIE, born 1837, daughter of Colin Horne {1808-1847}
and Margaret McHardy {1813-1900}, died in New York 2.1864.
[Longforgan g/s]

HORNE, THOMAS, born 1840, son of Colin Horne {1808-1847} a
gardener in Balrudderry, and Margaret McHardy {1813-1900},
died in Jersey City, USA, 2.1879. [Longforgan g/s]

HOULISTON, GEORGE, born 1778, died in Willoughby, Lake
County, Ohio, 6.1858. [Fogo g/s]

HOUSTON, JOHN MONTGOMERY, son of William Houston {1813-
1879} and Margaret Hamilton {1812-1893}, died in Canada West
29.9.1869. [Johnstone g/s]

HOWAT, CHARLES DOUGLAS, son of Alexander Howat {1770-
1834} and Elizabeth McGuffog, died in Kingston, Canada, aged
28. [Dumfries g/s]

HOWAT, ISABELLA, daughter of Alexander Howat {1770-1834} and
Elizabeth McGuffog, wife of Richard Jarrett, died in Hoboken
aged 57. [Dumfries g/s]

HOWDEN, JOHN, born 1783, son of Archibald Howden and Joan
Manderson, died in Savannah, North America, 26.10.1806.
[St Monance g/s]

HOWIE, ISABELLA, born 1839, daughter of John Howie {1806-1861}
and Ann Drysdale {1805-1851}, died in Hamilton, Ontario,
14.9.1875. [Edinburgh, Grange, g/s]

HUNTLY, MARY, born 1789, died in America 17.5.1856.
[Stichill g/s]

HUNTER, DANIEL, born 1864, died in Newport, Rhode Island,
15.12.1894. [Newton on Ayr g/s]

HUNTER, DAVID, born 1844, son of Samuel Hunter and Christina
Gibson, died in America 14.12.1889. [Dalry g/s]

HUNTER, DAVID, born 1846, son of William Hunter and Susan
Greig, died in Boston, Massachusetts, 28.2.1882.
[Brechin Cathedral g/s]

HUNTER, EDWARD, born 1819, son of Andrew Hunter and
Margaret Irons, died in Montreal 20.9.1847. [Dunnichen g/s]

HUNTER, GEORGE, son of John Hunter {1776-1856}, a surgeon,
died in Lapoela, Newfoundland, 6.7.1854. [Polwarth g/s]

HUNTER, GRACE GRIERSON, born 1865, daughter of David Hunter
and Janet Hamilton, wife of Robert L. Anderson, died in
Ekalaka, Montana, 28.1.1897. [Anwoth g/s]

HUNTER, JAMES, born 1849, died in Mobile, Alabama 31.1.1886.
[St Andrews g/s]

HUNTER, JOHN, died in Montreal 1890. [Paisley, Woodside, g/s]

HUNTER, THOMAS, son of Hugh Hunter and Mary Ramsay, died in America 4.1899. [Brechin Cathedral g/s]

HUNTER, WILHELMINA JANE, born 1830, daughter of Samuel Hunter and Christina Gibson, died in Guelph, Canada West, 8.9.1868. [Dalry g/s]

HUTCHISON, CATHERINE, born 1782, died in Clarke, Canada West, 27.9.1852. [Lanark g/s]

HUTCHISON, WILLIAM ORROCK, son of John Hutchison and Catherine ..., died in Toronto 25.5.1852. [Perth, Wellshill, g/s]

HUTTON, MARY, born 1816, daughter of David Hutton, wife of Robert Hood, died in California 25.1.1854. [Cupar g/s]

HUTTON, WILLIAM A., died in Florida 3.8.1896. [Dundee, Constitution Road, g/s]

INGLIS, ALEXANDER, born in Montrose 5.3.1814, Principal of the Prince of Wales College, Charlottetown, Canada, died in Kilmarnock 7.4.1894. [Kilmarnock g/s]

INGLIS, ALEXANDER, born 1860, son of David Inglis and Elizabeth Inglis, died in Valley Falls, New York, 14.1.1874. [Montrose, Rosehill, g/s]

INGLIS, JANE FARQUHAR, born 1867, daughter of David Inglis and Elizabeth Inglis, died in Valley Falls, New York, 16.4.1874. [Montrose, Rosehill, g/s]

INGLIS, JOHN, born 1805, son of William Inglis {1775-1833} Excise Supervisor in Teviotdale and Jane Tweedie {1771-1850}, a surgeon, died in New York 1849. [Edinburgh, Greyfriars, g/s]

INGLIS, MARY, born 1886, daughter of George Inglis {1842-1919}, wife of George Cameron, died in Spokane, USA, 5.7.1909. [Avoch g/s]

INNES, ALEXANDER, born 1806, son of John Innes and Ann Gunn, died in St Thomas, North America, 18.7.1848. [Golspie g/s]

INNES, CHARLES LAUDER, born 20.11.1842, son of Alexander M. Innes and Charlotte Lauder, died at Lake Oregon, USA, 19.3.1908. [Ayton g/s]

INNES, DAVID KENNEDY, born 1843, son of David Innes and Elizabeth Stephens, died in Wyoming 15.8.1879. [Coldstream g/s]

INNES, DONALD, born 1834, son of John Innes and Jane Grant in
Newton of Glenlivet, died in Granite, Virginia, 15.2.1899.
[Inveraven Downan g/s]

INNES, JOHN R., died in Buffalo, USA, 3.11.1806. [Dunbar g/s]

INNES, JOHN, son of .... Innes and Mary Dawson, died in St John,
New Brunswick, 8.187.. [Knockando g/s]

IRELAND, GEORGE, born 1839, died in San Francisco 3.2.1864.
[Dundee, Western, g/s]

IRELAND, JAMES, born 1827, son of William Ireland and Euphemia
Rodger, died in East Oakland, California, 16.3.1884.
[Ferry Port on Craig g/s]

IRELAND, JOHN, born 1862, son of James Ireland and Elizabeth
Milne, died in Alleghany City, USA, 19.2.1891. [Catterline g/s]

IRVINE, JAMES, born 1810, son of James Irvine and Ann .... in
Quebec, died in Edinburgh 1.10.1820.
[Edinburgh, Greyfriars, g/s]

IRVINE, MALCOLM, son of Robert Irvine {1800-1860} and Helen
Loudoun {1807-1867}, died in New York.
[Edinburgh, Grange, g/s]

JACK, JAMES, born 1852, son of James Jack and Isabella Wilson,
died in Minnesota 28.3.1905. [Roberton g/s]

JACKSON, GEORGE, born 1793, son of James Jackson and Margaret
Bread, died in Baltimore 15.7.1830. [Burntisland g/s]

JACKSON, JAMES, a merchant in Newfoundland by 1845. [Dalry g/s]

JACKSON, JOSEPH, son of Thomas Jackson {1756-1827} and
Margaret Grimman {1762-1838}, settled in Montreal.
[Kilspindie g/s]

JAMIESON, JOHN, born in Abington 22.6.1794, son of James
Jamieson and Mary Gillespie, partner in Gillespie Moffat and
Company of Montreal, died in Edinburgh, 1.1.1848. [Biggar g/s]

JAMIESON, MARION MCILWRAITH, daughter of John Jamieson
{1800-1873} and Elizabeth McIlwraith {1791-1875}, died in Ayr
1892, widow of John Barton Imrie, Columbus, Ohio.
[Colmonell g/s]

JARDINE, ANDREW, born 1848, son of James Jardine and Ann
Robertson, died 20.4.1872, buried in Laurelhill Cemetery,
Philadelphia. [Alexandria g/s]

JARVIS, ALEXANDER DUNCAN, born 1853, son of David Jarvis
and Margaret Buchanan, died in Boerne, Texas, 18.11.1882.
[Fettercairn g/s]

JEFFERSON, DAVID, son of John Jefferson {1806-1847} and Eliza
Ogilvy {1813-1863}, a shipmaster, drowned in San Francisco
16.9.1893, buried in Laurel Hill Cemetery there.
[Arbroath Abbey g/s]

JEFFREY, GEORGE, son of Peter Jeffrey, a blacksmith in Hopetoun,
{1780-1857}, and Agnes Kerr {1786-1846}, died in America
aged 47. [Abercorn g/s]

JOHANNES, JACOB, born in West Greenland 1811, died in Peterhead
21.3.1826. [Peterhead g/s]

JOHNSON, NELLY B., born 1870, wife of William M. Burnett, died
in Philadelphia 24.4.1896. [Peterculter g/s]

JOHNSON, WILLIAM, son of George Johnson, died in Chicago
31.10.1885. [Chirnside g/s]

JOHNSTON, ADAH, born 1858, wife of D. W. Cow, died in Montreal
21.7.1880. [Dundee, Western, g/s]

JOHNSTON, ALEXANDER, son of Adam Johnston in Crossrig
{1749-1828} and Janet Brown {1759-1817}, died in America.
[Whitsome g/s]

JOHNSTON, ALEXANDER, born 1810, a merchant in New York,
died in Patterson, New Jersey, 13.12.1846. [Balmaghie g/s]

JOHNSTON, ANN, born 1798, wife of William Stewart, died in
Andover, Massachusetts, 1.9.1855. [Farnell, Angus, g/s]

JOHNSTONE, ANN HARRIET, born 1842, daughter of Reverend
Thomas Johnstone and Margaret Adamson, wife of Reverend
W.M.Black, died in Montreal 21.10.1871. [Anwoth g/s]

JOHNSTON, ELISABETH, born 1855, daughter of George Johnston
and Rebecca Russell, died in Fitchburg, Massachusetts,
7.5.1902. [Ayton g/s]

JOHNSTON, JAMES, born 1769, in Outbrecks, Stenness, former
carpenter in Hudson Bay Company service, died 17.4.1842.
[Stenness g/s]

JOHNSTON, JANE, born 1818, wife of William Smart, died in
Andover, Massachusetts, 1.9.1855. [Farnell g/s]

JOHNSTON, JOHN, born 1782, son of John Johnston {1750-1841} miller at the Haugh of Urr, and Dorothea Proudfoot {1758-1794}, died in Patterson, New Jersey, 13.12.1846. [Balmaghie g/s]

JOHNSTON, JOHN, born 1782, died in New York 16.4.1851. [Balmaghie g/s]

JOHNSTON, JOSEPH, son of Adam Johnston in Crossrig {1749-1828} and Janet Brown {1759-1817}, died in America. [Whitsome g/s]

JOHNSTON, ROBERT, born 1791, son of Robert Johnston {1760-1838} a weaver in Greenlaw, and Isobel Black {1759-1813}, died in America 1.1830. [Greenlaw g/s]

JOHNSTON, ROBERT, born 1804, a merchant in New York, died in Paterson, New Jersey, 28.6.1848. [Balmaghie g/s]

JOHNSTONE, ROBERT ADAMSON, born 1847, son of Reverend Thomas Johnstone and Margaret Adamson, died in Montreal 11.4.1900. [Anwoth g/s]

JOHNSTON, WILLIAM, born 1807, a house carpenter, son of John Johnston and Jane Davidson, died in Quincy, Illinois, 29.6.1839. [Echt g/s]

JOLLY, JANE, born 1847, daughter of John Jolly and Mary Duncan, wife of Robert Durward, died in Preston, Ontario, 25.3.1922. [Montrose, Rosehill, g/s]

KAY, DAVID, born 1848, son of Reverend Cathcart Kay and Elizabeth McWilliam, died in Loup City, Nebraska, 9.7.1915. [Old Dailly g/s]

KEDSLIE, JOHN A., born 1872, son of John Kedslie {1846-1902} and Margaret McNellan, died in New Orleans 16.2.1891. [South Leith g/s]

KEEL, ISABELLA, born 1820, died in Thurald, Upper Canada, 18.1.1865. [West Linton g/s]

KEILLER, JESSIE BENNET, born 1802, died in Dundee 24.5.1843, wife of Robert Hood a merchant in Missouri. [Dundee, Howff, g/s]

KELLY, PHILIP, born 1818, died in New Orleans 10.1860. [Dalbeattie g/s]

KENNEDY, DAVID, born 1773, son of Thomas Kennedy and Ann Gibb, a merchant in Philadelphia, died in Germantown, Pennsylvania, 1798. [Falkland g/s]

KENNEDY, DAVID, son of ... Kennedy {1796-1847}, died in USA 3.1851. [Farnell g/s]

KENNEDY, CHARLES, born 1848, son of James Kennedy and Margaret Spalding, died in Hilo, Hawaii, 9.1.1919. [Kirriemuir g/s]

KENNEDY, JAMES, son of .... Kennedy {1796-1847}, died in New York 10.1896. [Farnell g/s]

KENNEDY, JOHN, born 1848, son of James Kennedy and Margaret Spalding, died in Redwood City, California, 20.4.1890. [Kirriemuir g/s]

KENNEDY, JOHN STEWART, son of ..... Kennedy {1796-1847}, died in USA 3.1871. [Farnell g/s]

KENNEDY, PETER, born 1849, son of Hugh Kennedy {1811-1876} a farmer and Janet McCosh {1813-1910}, died in Buckingham, Iowa, 28.2.1871. [Colmonell g/s]

KENNEDY, WILLIAM, son of James Kennedy {1805-1869} a miller and Janet Reay {1805-1876}, died in America aged 32. [Kirkgunzeon g/s]

KERR, ALEXANDER, son of ... Kerr and Betty Couttie {1796-1873}, settled in St John, New Brunswick. [Inverarity g/s]

KERR, CHARLES, born 1852, son of Charles M. Kerr, died in Manitoba 11.10.1883. [Edinburgh, St Cuthbert's, g/s]

KERR, JAMES, born 1797, son of William Kerr and Isobel Cuthill, died in Mobile, USA, 1831. [Fordoun g/s]

KERR, ROBERT, born 1829, son of Robert Kerr and Agnes Haldane, a Congregationalist minister in Tonah, Kansas, died in Wakefield, Kansas. 29.6.1890. [Kilmarnock g/s]

KEY, WILLIAM INGLIS, born 1816, son of John Key, died in New Orleans 5.4.1868. [Crail g/s]

KIDD, GEORGE WIGHTON, born 7.3.1849, son of William Kidd {1819-1868} and Ann Wighton {1823-1913}, died in Homestead, Pennsylvania, 3.3.1888. [Dundee, Eastern Necropolis, g/s]

KIDSTONE-KERR, JAMES, died in Virginia 8.1903. [Cleish g/s]

KING, ALEXANDER, son of John King {died 1844} and Margaret Warden {died 1825}, settled in Montreal. [Gourock g/s]

KING, WARDEN, in Montreal, son of John King {died 1844} and Margaret Warden {died 1823}. [Chapel St., Gourock, g/s]

KINLEYSIDE, ROBERT, born 1814, son of John Kinleyside {1780-1861} and Hellen Thompson {1779-1851}, died in Labrador 14.1.1850. [Whitsome g/s]

KINLOCH, CHARLES YOUNG, last of Gourdie, born 8.9.1863, died in Vernon, Canada, 26.3.1930. [Clunie g/s]

KINLOCH, CHRISTINA, born 1842, daughter of Archibald Kinloch and Ann David, died in Patterson, New Jersey, 117.2.1881. [Alexandria g/s]

KINNEAR, JAMES, born 6.3.1824, son of Archibald Kinnear and Jean Kinnear, died in Beardstown, Perry County, Tennessee, 3.3.1853. [Montrose, Rosehill, g/s]

KINNEAR, JOHN MCEWAN, died in Idaho 19.7.1890. [Dundee, Western, g/s]

KIRK, CATHERINE, born 1821, daughter of David Kirk and Janet Walker, died in America 1856. [Burntisland g/s]

KIRK, JAMES, son of James Kirk and Elspeth Russell, a merchant, settled in St John, New Brunswick, before 1832. [Pittenweem g/s]

KIRK, JOHN BALFOUR, born 3.4.1863, son of John Balfour Kirk MD {1826-1882} and Jessie Ingram Arthur {1829-1897}, died 11.8.1888, buried in Fairview Cemetery, Stillwater, USA. [Bathgate, Boghead, g/s]

KIRKWOOD, JAMES, won of William Kirkwood and Isabella Cockburn, died in Montreal 25.1.1870. [Musselburgh g/s]

KIRKWOOD, WILLIAM, born 1827, died in Chicago 15.11.1907. [Musselburgh g/s]

KISSOCK, THOMAS TWINAME, born 1863, son of William Kissock and Margaret Twiname, died in New Haven, Connecticut, 13.4.1907. [Crossmichael g/s]

KISSOCK, WILLIAM, born 1807, son of William Kissock and Mary Thomson, died in Litchburg, Virginia, 17.9.1842. [Crossmichael g/s]

KITCHEAN, JAMES, born 25.12.1797, a minister in Belleville, Canada, 1831-, died in Mordington 30.11.1871. [Mordington g/s]

KNIGHT, ISABELL, born 1801, daughter of David Knight and Margaret Clark, died in Illinois 24.9.1851. [Fetteresso g/s]

KNOX, MARY, born 1851, daughter of William Knox {1817-1875} and Margaret Cram {1824-1894}, died in Toronto 7.9.1874. [Crosbie g/s]

KNOX, THOMAS, born 1865, son of William Knox {1817-1875} and Margaret Cram {1824-1894}, died in Brazil, Indiana, 28.8.1896. [Crosbie g/s]

KNOX, WILLIAM, born 1781, son of William Knox {1743-1804} glazier in Edinburgh, and Janet Howden {1751-1822}, died in Philadelphia 1806. [St Cuthbert's, Edinburgh, g/s]

KYD, WILLIAM, born 1847, son of David Kyd and Ann Stewart, died in Troy, New York, 6.8.1891. [Arbroath Abbey g/s]

LAIDLAW, ADAM, born 10.9.1810, son of William Laidlaw {1760-1835}, in Horseburgh Castle, and Sarah Anderson {1780-1827}, died in Morpeth, Canada, 13.5.1855. [Innerleithen g/s]

LAIDLAW, ROBERT, born 3.12.1813, son of William Laidlaw {1760-1835}, in Horseburgh Castle, and Sarah Anderson {1780-1827}, died in Raleigh, Canada, 13.5.1855. [Innerleithen g/s]

LAIDLAW, THOMAS, son of Thomas Laidlaw {1749-1814} and Margaret Henderson {1764-1818}, died in Ohio 16.1.1851. [Ashkirk g/s]

LAING, DAVID, born 1849, son of Robert Laing and Margaret Millar, died in Hartford, USA, 18.12.1870. [Alyth g/s]

LAIRD, MARY. wife of James Houston, died in Mobile Bay 14.2.1858. [Port Glasgow g/s]

LAIRD, ROBERT, born 1837, son of William Laird {1801-1873} and Annie McDonald {1799-1883}, died in Dunville, Pennsylvania, 2.8.1870. [Dundee, Trottick, g/s]

LAMBIE, WILLIAM, born 1783, son of John Lambie {1755-1817} a stonemason, and Janet Torrance {1760-1844}, died in America 1854. [Kilmarnock g/s]

LAMONT, DANIEL, born in Greenock 10.4.1798, died in Lafayette, Missouri, 27.1.1837. [Greenock g/s]

LAMONT, DUNCAN, born in Greenock 31.10.1792, died in Brooklyn, New York, 8.3.1873. [Greenock g/s]

LAMONT, ELLEN FRANCES, born 1835, daughter of Daniel Lamont (above), died in Philadelphia 28.10.1881. [Greenock g/s]

LAMONT, WILLIAM, born 1821, son of William Lamont feuar in Port Bannatyne and Jean Stewart, died in New Orleans 8.4.1864.

[Rothesay g/s]
LANDELL, GEORGE RICHARDSON, born 1785, son of Reverend
James Landell and Janet Heriot, Lieutenant of the Royal
Marines, died in Montreal 8.8.1834. [Coldingham g/s]
LANG, THOMAS, son of Thomas Lang a merchant in Greenock,
shipmaster, 'lost at sea 1782', wife Mary Lewis of Virginia, died
in Virginia 1826. [Inverkip g/s]
LATOU, ROBERT, son of Peter Latou and Janet Henderson, settled in
New York before 1851. [Leuchars g/s]
LAUDER, GEORGE, son of John Lauder{1773-1857} and Isabella
Lyal {1772-1841}, settled in North Carolina. [Dalkeith New g/s]
LAUDER, JAMES HERVEY, son of John Lauder {died 1832} and
Jane Hervey {died 1832}, settled in Montreal before 1846.
[Greenock g/s]
LAUDER, JOHN ALEXANDER, born 1849, died in Elphinstone,
Manitoba, 27.9.1897. [Monzievaird g/s]
LAURENCE, ALEXANDER, son of Alexander Laurence {1796-1873}
and Ann Longmuir {1806-1876}, died in USA 13.9.18...
[Dunnottar g/s]
LAURIE, GEORGE, born 1834, son of William Laurie {1798-1870}
and Janet Brown {1799-1873}, died in Louisville, Kentucky,
8.5.1858. [Dunbar g/s]
LAURIE, JOHN, born 1873, son of William Laurie and Janet Skinner,
died in Toronto 14.8.1896. [Corsbank g/s]
LAW, ANN, born 1823, daughter of Andrew Law and Jane
McIlwraith, died in America 21.3.1866. [Girvan g/s]
LAW, INELLAN, daughter of William Law and Betty Ferrier, settled
in New York by 1889. [Farnell g/s]
LAW, JAMES, son of William Law and Betty Ferrier, settled in New
York by 1869. [Farnell g/s]
LAW, PETER, son of William Law and Betty Ferrier, settled in New
York by 1869. [Farnell g/s]
LAW, WILLIAM, son of William Law and Betty Ferrier, settled in
New York by 1869. [Farnell g/s]
LAWRENCE, WILLIAM, born in Blackford 1822, settled in
Merrimac, Iowa, died in Auchterarder 9.12.1889.
[Blackford g/s]

LAWSON, GEORGE, born 1859, son of Robert Lawson {1818-1899},
joiner in Coupar Angus, and Jane McKenzie {1822-1888}, died
in Cleveland, USA, 7.5.1898. [Coupar Angus g/s]

LAWSON, JOHN, born 1795, son of ...Lawson and Jean Hynd {1768-
1822}, died in New Orleans 1822. [Dundee, Howff, g/s]

LAWSON, THOMAS, born 1850, son of Robert Lawson {1818-1899},
joiner in Coupar Angus, and Jane McKenzie {1822-1888}, died
in San Antonio, Texas, 2.5.1883. [Coupar Angus g/s]

LAWSON, WILLIAM, born 1819, late a blacksmith in Bankhill,
Countesswells, died in Camperdown, Canada, 7.1.1897.
[Peterculter g/s]

LAYTON, DAVID STARK, born 1813, son of Thomas Layton,
surgeon and medical superintendent in Isle of Maintowaning,
Upper Canada, died 25.10.1866. [Kinross, Kirkgate, g/s]

LECKIE, JOHN, born 1835, son of William Leckie and Eleanor
McFarlan, died in Manitoba 1895. [Kippen g/s]

LEES, HENRY, born 1839, son of James Lees, died in Chicago 1867.
[Kilconquhar g/s]

LEES, JOHN, born 1804, son of John Lees and Jean Young, died in
Chelsea, Boston, Massachusetts, 4.3.1878. [Galashiels g/s]

LEGGAT, ANDREW, born 1805, son of Andrew Leggat {1780-1827}
a whip manufacturer and Helen Hume {1774-1837}, died in New
York 1.6.1827. [Edinburgh, Greyfriars, g/s]

LEGGAT, DAVID, born 1810, son of Alexander Leggat and
Wilhelmina Hutchison, died in New York 16.12.1842.
[Edinburgh, St Cuthbert's, g/s]

LEGGAT, GIDEON, born 1791, son of James Leggat {1764-1845} and
Mary Wilson {1768-1818}, died in Virginia 1838.
[Edinburgh, New Calton, g/s]

LEIGHTON, MATTHEW, born 1818, son of Miles Leighton and
Elizabeth Ridley, died in Boston, USA, 26.7.1854.
[Dumfries g/s]

LEIPER, JOHN, born 1835, son of William Leiper and Jane Hamilton,
minister of Barrie Presbyterian Church, Ontario, died
31.12.1886. [Newmilns g/s]

LEISHMAN, Reverend WILLIAM, born in Falkirk 1.5.1785, a
merchant in Halifax, Nova Scotia, died in Edinburgh 31.10.1871.
[Edinburgh, New Calton, g/s]

LEITCH, Reverend WILLIAM, born 1815, for 18 years Principal of
Queen's College, Kingston, Canada, died in Monimail 9.5.1864,
husband of Euphemia Paterson. [Monimail g/s]

LEITCH, WILLIAM, born 1826, son of Alexander Leitch and
Elizabeth Petrie, a merchant, died in Montreal 14.2.1876.
[Guthrie g/s]

LEITH, ALBERT HOWE, born in Aberdeen 1.6.1851, son of John
Leith, a resident of Australia, USA, and Mexico, died in
Cornwall 6.1902. [Fyvie g/s]

LENNOX, JANE, born 1887, daughter of Robert Lennox and Jane
Lennox, died in Braddock, Alleghany County, Pennsylvania,
16.7.1891. [Patna g/s]

LEONARD, HUGH, son of Patrick Leonard {died 1843} and Ann
Dawson {died 1893}, settled in Pittsburgh, America.
[Kilmarnock g/s]

LESLIE, ALEXANDER, born 1765, son of Andrew Leslie and Jean
Orrock, died in America 1818. [Burntisland g/s]

LESLIE, JOHN, born 1772, son of Andrew Leslie and Jean Orrock,
died in America 1818. [Burntisland g/s]

LESLIE, PETER, born 1820, died in Inland, Adams County,
Nebraska, 12.7.1872. [Arbroath Abbey g/s]

LESLIE, THOMAS, son of James Leslie {1813-1892} and Isabel
Shearer {1825-1915}, died at Lake Michigan 7.11.1872.
[Stronsay, St Peter's, g/s]

LESLY, DAVID, son of David Lesly and Jane Kinnear, settled in New
York as a shipmaster before 1826. [Monimail g/s]

LESSELS, GEORGE, born 1825, son of George Lessels and Martha
Henderson, died in America 1847. [Newburgh g/s]

LETHAM, JOHN, died in New York 30.3.1901.
[Edinburgh, New Calton, g/s]

LEYS, GEORGE, born 1834, son of John Leys, farmer in Scallie, and
Mary Duthie, died in New Orleans 20.10.1848. [Udny g/s]

LIDDLE, JOHN, born 1829, died in Glenallen, Canada, 19.4.1880.
[Wiston g/s]

LINDSAY, ANDREW, born 1804, a skipper in Montrose, died in
Quebec 25.5.1845. [Craig Inchbrioch g/s]

LINDSAY, ANN, born 1779, wife of Patrick Glenday {1777-1836},
died in St Charles, Missouri, 3.11.1821. [Rattray g/s]

LINDSAY, DAVID, born 1840, son of John Lindsay and Betsy
Mackie, died in Rochester, America, 1875. [Edzell g/s]

LINDSAY, GEORGE, born 1850, son of John Lindsay and Eliza
Hunter, died in Richmond, Virginia, 13.4.1906. [Lauder g/s]

LINDSAY, JAMES, born 1794, a joiner, son of John Lindsay and
Margaret Jackson, died in New Orleans 28.8.1822.
[Falkland g/s]

LINDSAY, JAMES, born 1815, son of Robert Lindsay {1783-1864}
and Jean Lindsay {1788-1852}, died in New York 18.8.1848.
[Kirriemuir g/s]

LINDSAY, JOHN, born 1801, son of John Lindsay and Margaret
Jackson, a joiner, died in New York 22.5.1855. [Falkland g/s]

LINDSAY, JOHN, born 1838, died in Will County, Illinois,
24.12.1871. [Fenwick g/s]

LINDSAY, JOHN, born 1870, son of John Lindsay and Elizabeth
Esplin, died in Ionapah, Nevada, 28.10.1918. [Thankerton g/s]

LISTON, JAMES, son of James Liston {died 1853} and Isobel Soutar
{died 1863}, died in Montreal 8.1.1867. [Lethendy g/s]

LITHGOW, ALEXANDER RONALD, born 1865, son of Thomas
Lithgow and Isabella Shaw, died in Pittsburgh, Pennsylvania,
1.6.1915, buried in Highwood Cemetery, Pittsburgh.
[Lanark g/s]

LITTLE, CHARLES, born 1822, son of William Little {1774-1852}
and Agnes Little {1785-1852}, a baker, died in New York 1861.
[Cavers g/s]

LIVINGSTONE, A.C., son of Archibald Livingstone, {1781-1857},
coastwaiter at the Isle of Whithorn, died in Jacksonville, Florida,
aged 68. [Whithorn g/s]

LIVINGSTONE, HUGH, born 1811, died in Port Hope, Upper
Canada, 12.1.1831. [Crossmichael g/s]

LOCHEAD, ISABELLA, born 1833, daughter of Robert Lochead and
Janet Thomson, wife of John Howat, died in Canada 1.4.1869.
[Galston g/s]

LOGAN, DANIEL, born 1805, died in the State of New York
21.5.1872. [Edrom g/s]

LOGAN, JAMES, in Worcester, Massachusetts, grandson of James
Logan {1778-1860} and Margaret Thompson {1783-1825}.
[Lochwinnoch g/s]

LOGIE, WILLIAM, Major of the United States Army, son of
Alexander Logie {1756-1836} and Agnes Cluny {1757-1823} in
Fochabers. [Speymouth, Essil g/s]

LORIMER, HENRY JAMES, born 1854, son of George Lorimer and
Margaret Wilkie, died in San Jose, California, 17.9.1891.
[Edinburgh, St Cuthbert's, g/s]

LOW, ALEXANDER, son of James Low {died 1819} and Ann
Fairweather {died 1858}, a merchant in Mexico around 1858.
[Dundee, Constitution Road, g/s]

LOW, JAMES, son of James Low {1794-1859} and Elizabeth Young
{died 1831}, settled in Salt Lake City, USA, by 1881.
[Stirling, Holy Rude, g/s]

LOWE, WILLIAM SHIRESS, born 1826, son of David Lowe and Jane
Christison, died in Batty Park, Isle of Wight County, Virginia,
7.3.1903. [Brechin Cathedral g/s]

LUNDIE, MARY, born 1841, daughter of Andrew Lundie and Jane
Ruxton, died in Denver, Colorado, 30.7.1885.
[Arbroath Abbey g/s]

LYALL, JAMES, son of James Lyall {1792-1858}, settled in Andover,
Massachusetts. [Brechin Cathedral g/s]

LYON, DAVID, born 1801, son of William Lyon and Barbara Wattie,
died in Varna, Canada West, 12.8.1876. [Strathcathro g/s]

LYON, JEAN, born 1800, wife of Thomas Hamilton, died 21.11.1883,
buried in Greenwood cemetery, New York. [Newmilns g/s]

LYON, JOHN, born 1765, a botanist, died in Nashville, North
Carolina, 14.8.1814. [Dundee, Howff, g/s]

MCALPINE, DANIEL CURRIE, born 1857, son of Robert McAlpine
{1814-1863} and Janet Currie {1818-1891}, died in Hoytdale,
Pennsylvania, 15.3.1903. [St Ninian's g/s]

MCBAIN, JOHN, born 1817, son of Lachlan McBain {1780-1857} a
tailor, and Margaret ...{1791-1869}, died in Teeswater, Canada,
28.7.1905. [Alvie g/s]

MCBAIN, JOHN, born 1831, son of Thomas McBain {1778-1855} and
Janet McIntyre {1791-1869}, 'late of Lucknow, Canada', died in
Drumguish 9.6.1904. [Rothiemurcus g/s]

MCBEAN, ALLAN, son of Allan McBean, farmer in Boggiewell, and
Catherine Mackay, died in Zortman, Montana, 8.1.1912.
[Suddie, Black Isle, g/s]

MCBEAN, BENJAMIN, son of John McBean {1826-1895} and Catherine Dean {1829-1895}, settled in America. [Rothiemurcus g/s]

MCBEAN, JAMES, son of John McBean {1826-1895} and Catherine Dean {1829-1895}, settled in America. [Rothiemurcus g/s]

MCBEAN, JOHN, son of John McBean {1826-1895} and Catherine Dean {1829-1895}, settled in America. [Rothiemurcus g/s]

MCBEATH, ADAM, son of Neil McBeath and Margaret Ross, died in Toronto 1880. [Clyne, Kirkton, g/s]

MCBEATH, JOHN, son of Neil McBeath and Margaret Ross, died in Toronto 1888. [Clyne, Kirkton, g/s]

MCBRYDE, JAMES, a merchant in Georgia, son of John McBryde, farmer in Little Tongus, and Margaret Donnan, {18..?}. [Whithorn g/s]

MCBRYDE, JOHN, a merchant in Georgia, son of John McBryde, a farmer in Little Tongue, and Margaret Donnan, {18..?}. [Whithorn g/s]

MCBRIDE, NEIL, born 1819, son of Alexander McBride {1774-1848} a farmer in Moniemore, and Mary .... {1782-1867}, died in South Hampton, Canada West, 6.4.1853. [Kilbride, Arran, g/s]

MCCALLUM, ISABELLA, born 1849, daughter of Duncan McCallum and Amelia Cruickshank, died in Kansas City, USA, 1.3.1899. [Fetteresso g/s]

MCCANN, JANE, born 1851, daughter of Charles McCann {1817-1865} and Mary Sweeney {1819-1854}, died in New York 1881. [Greenock g/s]

MCCAULL, JOHN, born 1822, son of James McCaull and Barbara Milwain, died in America 7.11.1858. [Monigaff g/s]

MCCAW, THOMAS, son of John McCaw and Mary Grange, a merchant in Montreal, died 10.1865. [Colmonell g/s]

MCCAW, WILLIAM, son of Robert McCaw {1827-1876} and Jessie McTier {1820-1901}, died in Richmond, Illinois, aged 68. [Colmonell g/s]

MCCLELLAND, JOHN, born 1810, son of John McClelland {1783-1835}, a merchant, died in Charleston, Illinois, 10.9.1842. [Wigtown g/s]

MCCLYMONT, JOHN, born 1850, son of John McClymont and Mary Rankin, died in New York 11.9.1905. [Maybole g/s]

MCCOLL, DUGALD D., born 1770, landed proprietor in Caledonia, New York, died 29.10.1818. [Keil Chapel in Appin g/s]

MCCOMBIE, RACHEL, wife of John Duthie, died in Los Animos, Colorado, 18.12.1891. [Tough g/s]

MCCONCHIE, DAVID, born 1809, died in Atlanta, Nebraska, 21.1.1893. [Monigaff g/s]

MCCONOCHIE, ALEXANDER, born 1803, son of William McConochie and Isabel Kerr, died in Brooklyn, New York, 9.5.1862. [Balmaghie g/s]

MCCOSH, JAMES, born in Garskeoch 1.4.1811, died in Princeton, New Jersey, 16.11.1894. [Straiton g/s]

MCCOUL, WILLIAM CAMPBELL, born 1824, son of David McCoul and Margaret Campbell, died in California 16.2.1850. [Crossmichael g/s]

MCCOWAN, WILLIAM, born 1817, soldier of the 58th Masschusetts Infantry, died at Camp Readville, USA, 1.4.1864. [Dunblane g/s]

MCCRAE, JOHN, son of James McCrae {1765-1839} and Janet Galbraith {1776-1857}, died in Paris, Canada West, 21.2.1845. [Carsphairn g/s]

MCCRAE, ROBERT, born 1809, son of James McCrae {1765-1839} and Janet Galbraith {1776-1857}, died in Colborn, America, 6.10.1869. [Carsphairn g/s]

MCCREDIE, WILLIAM, born 1806, a staff surgeon, died in Bermuda 13.10.1840. [Kirkcaldy g/s]

MCCREDIE, WILLIAM, born 1805, emigrated to Canada 1872, returned and died in Old Luce 15.5.1880. [Whithorn Old g/s]

MCCULLOCH, WILLIAM, born 1846, son of Henry McCulloch, died in Kansas 1.1.1912. [Kirkandrews g/s]

MCDADE, HUGH, born 1856, son of Robert McDade and Jessie McLachlan, died in Virginia City, Nevada, 10.7.1913. [Anwoth g/s]

MCDADE, JAMES, born 1854, son of Robert McDade and Jessie McLachlan, died in Virginia City, Nevada, 26.5.1886. [Anwoth g/s]

MCDADE, WILLIAM, born 1859, son of Robert McDade and Jessie McLachlan, died in Virginia City, Nevada, 7.1.1889. [Anwoth g/s]

MACDONALD, ALEXANDER, born in Forsie 30.12.1838, son of Neil MacDonald and Annie Bruce, died in America 13.8.1898. [Trostan Westfield g/s]

MCDONALD, ALEXANDER, born 1851, son of James McDonald and Margaret McGlashan, died in America 9.9.1872. [Blairgowrie g/s]

MACDONALD, ARCHIBALD, born 1854, son of William McDonald and Isabella Kennedy, died in Emden, Illinois, 14.5.1877. [Pollockshaws g/s]

MACDONALD, DONALD, born 1783, son of William MacDonald, farmer in Ballintuim Foss, and Isabella Stewart, a farmer in New Perth, Prince Edward Island, died 1867. [Struan g/s]

MCDONALD, FLORA, born 1722, late of North Carolina, died 3.1790. [Osmigarry g/s]

MCDONALD, HECTOR, born 1824, son of Hector McDonald and Helen McConochy, died in Montreal 4.11.1850. [Kingarth g/s]

MCDONALD, Sir JOHN, born in Ramshorn, Glasgow, 1815, emigrated to Kingston, Upper Canada, 1820, Prime Minister of Canada, died 1891. [Ramshorn MI]

MACDONALD, JOHN A., born in Windsor, Nova Scotia, 4.1807, a shipmaster, died in Port Bannatyne, Bute, 8.1863. [Greenock g/s]

MACDONALD, JOHN, in Oaklands, Toronto, grandson of Alexander MacDonald {1762-1828} and Jessie Fraser {1758-1838}. [Boleskine g/s]

MCDONALD, JOHN, born 1813, son of John McDonald and Jane Maule, died in Janetsville, Ontario, 27.11.1891. [Blairingone g/s]

MCDONALD, LEWIS, son of Alexander McDonald and Margaret Milne, died in Canada 1849. [Fraserburgh g/s]

MCDOUGALL, DUNCAN, son of Malcolm McDougall {1802-1832} and Ann Livingston {1804-1873}, died in Virginia City, Nevada, 28.4.1891. [Rothesay g/s]

MCEWAN, DUNCAN, born 1818, son of Hugh McEwan {1785-1834} a mason in Dunkeld, and Christine McCallum {1783-1861}, died in Detroit 27.7.1859. [Little Dunkeld g/s]

MCEWAN, EWAN, son of Alexander McEwan {1715-1797} a farmer in Keprannich and Janet McVichie {1736-1794}, settled in New York, died in Newtown, Killin, 21.9.1811.
[Kenmore Ardtainaig g/s]

MCEWAN, JOHN, Sergeant Major of H Company, 65rh Regiment of the Illinois Volunteer Infantry, died in the US Civil War 1861-1865. [Edinburgh, Old Calton, g/s]

MCEWAN, JOHN, born 1806, son of William McEwan, died in Mexico 1832. [Moneydie, Logiealmond, g/s]

MCEWAN, MARGARET, born 1823, wife of Robert McLauchlan, died in Flat Rock, North Carolina, 10.3.1886. [Buchlyvie g/s]

MCFADYEAN, COLL, born 1844, son of Duncan McFadyean, tacksman of Clenamackire and Susan Ann McIntyre, died in Buffalo 16.5.1865 from wounds received in the 13th action of the 5th Michigan Infantry in the US Civil War.
[Ardchattan Priory g/s]

MCFADYEAN, JOHN, born 1869, son of John McFadyean {1839-1917} and Lily McKie {1841-1927}, died in Lake Superior 17.8.1895. [Barr g/s]

MACFARLANE, DANIEL, born 1821, son of Alexander MacFarlane and Euphemia Watson, died in Montreal 29.12.1840.
[Perth, Greyfriars, g/s]

MACFARLANE, DAVID JOBSON, born 1817, son of Alexander MacFarlane, an ironfounder in Perth, and Euphemia Watson, died in Montreal 1866. [Perth, Greyfriars, g/s]

MACFARLANE, DONALD, born 1821, son of Alexander MacFarlane, {1763-1838} an ironfounder in Perth, and Euphemia Watson, {1778-1854}, died in Montreal 29.12.1840.
[Perth, Greyfriars, g/s]

MACFARLANE, HENRY HEPBURN, born 1813, son of Alexander Macfarlane, {1763-1838} an ironfounder in Perth, and Euphemia Watson, {1778-1854}, died in Alexandria, Canada, 1875.
[Perth, Greyfriars, g/s]

MCFARLANE, HUGH, born 1840, died in New York 15.4.1876.
[Edinburgh, St Cuthbert's, g/s]

MACFARLANE, HUGH, born 1860, son of Hugh MacFarlane {1816-1895} a manufacturer and banker, died in St Petersburg, Virginia, 14.6.1898. [Paisley, Woodside, g/s]

MACFARLANE, JAMES, born 1811, son of Alexander MacFarlane,
{1763-1838} an ironfounder in Perth, and Euphemia Watson,
{1778-1854}, died in Chicago, 1856. [Perth, Greyfriars, g/s]

MCFARLANE, JOHN, born 1857, son of Robert McFarlane and
Margaret Hastie, died in Montreal 7.9.1914. [Thankerton g/s]

MACFARLANE, NORMAN, born 1846, son of William MacFarlane,
clothier in Coupar Angus, and Elizabeth Will, died in Chicago
21.3.1892. [Coupar Angus g/s]

MACFARLANE, PETER, born 1819, son of Alexander MacFarlane,
{11816-1895} an ironfounder in Perth, and Euphemia Watson,
{1778-1854}, died in Montreal 1879. [Perth, Greyfriars, g/s]

MACFARLANE, WILLIAM STUART, born in Perth 12.1814, son of
Alexander Macfarlane, an ironfounder in Perth and Euphemia
Watson, died in Montreal 2.1885. [Perth, Greyfriars, g/s]

MCGHIE, FRANCIS ALEXANDER, born 20.11.1806 in Toull, died
in Tuscaloosa, Alabama, 20.8.1856. [Buittle g/s]

MCGIBBON, CHARLES, born 1843, died in New York 10.1.1872.
[Edinburgh, New Calton, g/s]

MCGIBBON, CHRISTINA, born 1800, wife of Reverend William
Rintoul in Montreal, died 7.8.1855.
[Edinburgh, New Calton, g/s]

MCGIBBON, FRANCES, wife of John McGibbon, late of
Newfoundland, died in Killin 5.11.1847. [Lawers g/s]

MCGIBBON, JOHN, son of Duncan McGibbon {1727-1812} and
Margaret Campbell {1737-1807}, died at sea between Jamaica
and Nova Scotia. [Amulree g/s]

MCGIBBON, JOSEPH, son of Duncan McGibbon {1727-1812} and
Margaret Campbell {1737-1807}, died at sea between Jamaica
and Nova Scotia. [Amulree g/s]

MCGIBBON, PATRICK, son of Duncan McGibbon {1727-1812} and
Margaret Campbell {1737-1807}, died at sea between Jamaica
and Nova Scotia. [Amulree g/s]

MCGILL, CATHERINE WILLMOT, born 1845, daughter of James
McGill and Janet Corson, wife of James Telfer, died in
McKeesport, Pennsylvania, 7.7.1915. [Dalry g/s]

MCGILL, JOHN, son of Donald McGill and Margaret McCutcheon,
died in Montreal 20.3.1850. [Monigaff g/s]

MCGILL, PETER, son of Donald McGill and Margaret McCutcheon, died in New York 21.2.1831. [Monigaff g/s]

MCGILL, WILLIAM MCCUTCHEON, born 1821, son of Donald McGill and Margaret McCutcheon, died in Simcoe, Canada, 2.8.1855. [Monigaff g/s]

MCGILLVRAY, ANN, born 1773, wife of Donald McIntosh, died in Columbiana County, Ohio, 4.2.1850. [Dalarossie Moy g/s]

MCGILLEVRIE, JOHN, born 1791, son of Peter McGillevrie {1755-1830}, a farmer, and Janet Robertson {1768-1838}, died in Richmond, Virginia. 1820. [Logierait g/s]

MCGREGOR, DAVID, born 1850, son of John McGregor and Mary Geddes, died in Hamilton, Canada, 26.3.1889. [Perth, Greyfriars, g/s]

MCGREGOR, DONALD, son of William McGregor {1794-1864} and Jane Gunn {1811-1838}, settled in Canada West. [Latheron Old g/s]

MCGREGOR, MARY, born 1873, wife of E.J.Runham, died in Calgary, North West Territory, 28.2.1901. [Kirkintilloch g/s]

MCGREGOR, ROBERT, born 1843, son of Donald McGregor and Margaret Sutherland, died in America 1894. [Latheron Old g/s]

MCHARDY, WILLIAM, born 1797, son of Charles McHardy {1745-1815} a schoolmaster and Henrietta Murray {1767-1819}, died in Savannah 22.9.1820. [Fetteresso g/s]

MCHOULL, ROBERT, son of William McHoull {1783-1848} a merchant in Galston, settled in Cartwright township, Canada, [Galston g/s]

MCLIWRAITH, JOHN, born 1808, son of David McIlwraith and Jane Gregg, died in New York 12.8.1845. [Barr g/s]

MCILWRAITH, MARGARET, daughter of John McIlwraith and Susanna Boag, died in Alma, Peel Township, Canada West, 30.6.1871. [Greenock, Inverkip Street, g/s]

MCILWRICK, DAVID, born 1814, son of David McIlwrick {1766-1832} and Helen McMurray {1779-1852}, died in Knoxville, USA, 21.4.1844. [Colmonell g/s]

MCINDOE, WALTER, son of Robert McIndoe in Carbeth, a merchant in Virginia. [Strathblane g/s]

MCINNES, WILLIAM, born 1845, son of Malcolm McInnes and Margaret Matheson, died in Canada 2.1917. [Lairg g/s]

MCINROY, CHARLES HESKETH, born 6.11.1860, son of William
McInroy of Lude, died in Spokane, USA, 8.11.1910.
[Kilmaveonaig g/s]

MCINROY, HENRY, born 1841, son of James Patrick McInroy of
Lude and Margaret Seaton Lillie, died in Colorado 12.6.1902.
[Kilmaveonaig g/s]

MCINROY, PATRICK, born 16.7.1845, son of James Patrick McInroy
of Lude and Margaret Seton Lillie, died in Pueblo, Colorado,
12.11.1882. [Kilmaveonaig g/s]

MCINTYRE, ALEXANDER, son of Alexander McIntyre {1795-1869}
and Isabella Falconer {1807-1883}, settled in Canada West by
1862. [Geddes g/s]

MCINTYRE, ELIZABETH MCLAREN, born 1807, daughter of
Donald McIntyre {1766-1856} a farmer in West Dundurcas and
Margaret Ferguson {1787-1875}, died in Canada 1837.
[Comrie g/s]

MCINTYRE, PETER, born 1815, son of Donald McIntyre and
Margaret Ferguson, died in Canada 1854. [Comrie g/s]

MCISAAC, JOHN, born 1805, late minister at Lochiell, Glengarry,
Upper Canda, died in Oban 15.1.1847. [Oban g/s]

MCIVER, ANN, born 1795, wife of Norman Campbell, died in
Brooklyn, New York, 5.5.1860. [Dingwall, St Clement's, g/s]

MCKAY, ADAM, son of Hugh McKay in Gruids {1782-1862}, settled
in America. [Lairg g/s]

MCKAY, ALEXANDER, born 1880, son of Murdo McKay {1842-
1895} and Elizabeth McHattie, died in Donara, USA, 9.9.1904.
[Killearnan g/s]

MACKAY, ANDREW, son of John Mackay {1786-1859} and Marion
Mackay {1799-1872}, settled as a carpenter in West Zora,
Canada. [Dornoch g/s]

MACKAY, ANGUS, born 1844, son of Donald Mackay and Ann
Matheson, died in New York 19.1.1904. [Dornoch g/s]

MACKAY, CATHERINE, born 1850, daughter of John Mackay and
Catherine Forbes, died in Memphis, Tennessee, 1878.
[Latheron Old g/s]

MACKAY, CHRISTINE MCINTOSH LESLIE, born 1853, daughter
of Donald Mackay and Mary Ross, died in Toledo, Illinois,
24.11.1899. [Durness g/s]

MACKAY, GEORGE SINCLAIR, born 1863, son of James Mackay
and Jessie Sutherland, died in Oklahoma City 2.9.1889.
[Halkirk g/s]
MACKAY, HUGH, born 1833, son of Eric Mackay, died in Canada
5.1881. [Durness g/s]
MACKAY, HUGH, born 1870, son of John Mackay and mary Gunn,
died in Astoria, Long Island, 4.2.1907. [Strathy, Sutherland, g/s]
MCKAY, JANET, daughter of William McKay {1788-1846} and Anne
McKay {1793-1883}, wife of ... Ross, settled in Ontario.
[Farr g/s]
MACKAY, JOHN, son of George Mackay {1779-1837} and Catherine
Mackay {1793-1854}, an Inspector of the *Detroit and Milwaukee
Railroad.* [Farr g/s]
MCKAY, WILLIAM, son of Hugh McKay in Gruids {1782-1862},
settled in America. [Lairg g/s]
MACKAY, WILLIAM, born 1836, son of John Mackay and Elizabeth
Budge, died in South Carolina 25.8.1874. [Dunnet g/s]
MACKAY, WILLIAM, born 1834, died in Portage la Prairie,
Manitoba, 25.7.1924. [Rogart g/s]
MACKAY, WILLIAM, born 1867, died in Philadelphia 10.3.1889.
[Strathy, Sutherland, g/s]
MCKEAN, ALEXANDER CHARLES, son of William Blair MacKean
{1799-1875} and Marianne McCulloch, died in San Francisco
8.1869. [Edinburgh, Greyfriars, g/s]
MCKEAN, ELIZABETH, daughter of James McKean {1818-1886}
and Mary Gemmill {1819-1872}, died in New York 26.10.1889.
[Paisley Woodside g/s]
MCKEAND, ADAM, born 1818, son of Adam McKeand and Marion
McCartney, died in Madison, Indiana, 7.7.1849. [Monigaff g/s]
MCKEE, CHRISTINA, born in Cornwall, Glengarry County, Upper
Canada, 25.4.1819, wife of Peter Ireland, died in Perth
14.11.1849. [Perth, Greyfriars, g/s]
MACKENZIE, COLIN, son of John Mackenzie {1827-1875} and Ann
Mackenzie {1826-1921}, settled in Detroit. [Creich g/s]
MACKENZIE, COLQUHOUN, born 1786, son of Alexander
Mackenzie {1739-1825} tenant in Easter Duthil, and Anne
McQueen {1758-1845}, died in Quebec 30.8.1828. [Duthil g/s]

MCKENZIE, GEORGE, son of .... McKenzie and Isabel Cameron
{1789-1871}, settled in Canada West. [Dornoch g/s]

MACKENZIE, HUGH, born 1845, son of Alexander MacKenzie and
Christine Grant, chief officer of the US barque Solomon, died in
San Francisco 10.12.1873. [Golspie g/s]

MCKENZIE, JAMES KAY, born 1836, son of William McKenzie and
Elizabeth Kay, died in North Portal, Saskatoon, Canada,
27.2.1916. [Dundee, Balgay, g/s]

MACKENZIE, JOHN, born 1860, son of Donald MacKenzie and
Margaret Gunn, died in New Brunswick 18.4.1862. [Latheron
Old g/s]

MACKENZIE, JOHN, son of Donald MacKenzie {1758-1846} a
farmer in Balnagra and Ann MacKenzie {1773-1854}, settled in
California. [Lochcarron g/s]

MACKENZIE, JOHN, born 1861, a blacksmith, son of John
MacKenzie {1810-1884} and Anne McGregor {1830-1918}, died
in Cincinatti 17.7.1887. [Annat, Ross & Cromarty, g/s]

MCKENZIE, NORMAN, born 1848, son of Alexander McKenzie and
Jane MacRae, died in Kenona, Canada, 12.1910. [Stoer g/s]

MCKENZIE, ROBERT, born 1803, '21 years in America', died in
Leslie 24.4.1854. [Leslie g/s]

MACKENZIE, RODERICK, son of John Mackenzie {1778-1825} in
Balnagro, a merchant in Cape Breton. [Lochcarron g/s]

MACKENZIE, RODERICK, son of Alexander McKenzie {died 1802},
Chief Factor of the Hudson Bay Company. [Lochinver g/s]

MACKENZIE, WILLIAM, born 1851, son of William Mackenzie
{1818-1879} and Elizabeth Kay {1817-1889}, died in Paterson,
New Jersey, 6.1.1896. [Dundee, Balgay, g/s]

MCKERCHAR, ALEXANDER, son of Duncan McKerchar {1775-
1835} and Mary Stewart {1787-1870}, settled in Washington,
D.C. [Fortingall g/s]

MCKERCHAR, DONALD, born 1856, son of Donald McKerchar and
Isabella McGregor, died in Minnepolis 4.2.1917.
[Fortingall Kerrowmore g/s]

MCKERCHAR, WILLIAM, son of Duncan McKerchar {1775-1835}
and Mary Stewart {1787-1870}, settled in Wroxeter, Canada.
[Fortingall g/s]

MACKIE, AGNES, born 1847, daughter of John Mackie and Mary
Clark, died in Detroit 9.7.1875. [Arbroath Abbey g/s]
MCKIE, ALEXANDER, born 1818, died in Sheldon, Houstoun,
Minnesota, 27.12.1866. [Barr g/s]
MCKIE, ANNIE, born 1834, daughter of David McKie and Jane
Dalziel, died in America 2.3.1857. [Dalry g/s]
MACKIE, DAVID, born 1764, son of Thomas Mackie and Margaret
Louden, died in Savannah 1794. [Colvend g/s]
MACKIE, ISABELLA, born 1845, daughter of John Mackie and Mary
Clark, died in Detroit 15.2.1879. [Arbroath Abbey g/s]
MCKIE, PETER, son of James McKie {1725-1789} and Agnes Wilson,
settled in Philadelphia. [Dumfries g/s]
MCKIE, WILLIAM, born 1808, son of William McKie and Janet
McMurray, died in Illinois 14.9.1847. [Barr g/s]
MCKIE, WILLIAM, son of James McKie {1725-1789} and Agnes
Wilson, settled in Philadelphia. [Dumfries g/s]
MCKIE, WILLIAM, born 1848, son of John McKie and Isabel
Maxwell, died in Cornland, Illinois, 7.2.1911. [Kirkandrews g/s]
MCKINLAY, HANNAH GRACE, born 1844, daughter of John
McKinlay and Mary Mitchell, died in Newfoundland 17.3.1850.
[Rothesay g/s]
MCKINLAY, JOHN, born 4.1850, son of John McKinlay and Mary
Mitchell, died in Newfoundland 28.10.1850. [Rothesay g/s]
MCKINLAY, JOHN EDWARD, born 1847, son of John McKinlay and
Mary Mitchell, died in Newfoundland 14.12.1849.
[Rothesay g/s]
MCKINNON, DONALD, born 1817, a farmer from Urchary, Beauly,
died in America 20.6.1888. [Beauly Priory g/s]
MCKNIGHT, ALEXANDER, born 1830, son of Robert McKnight and
Jane McLean, died in Gothenburg, Nebraska, 25.1.1897.
[Buittle g/s]
MCLAGGAN, JOHN, born 1807, son of James McLaggan and
Elizabeth Ireland {1778-1816}, died in St John, New Brunswick,
20.1.1820.[Balmaghie g/s]
MCLAREN, DANIEL, son of Daniel McLaren and Jane Crawford,
President of *the Cincinatti, Hamilton and Dayton Railroad*, died
in Glendale, Hamilton, Ohio, 9.9.1875. [Dundee, Western, g/s]

MCLAREN, DUNCAN, son of Donald McLaren and Margaret
McGregor, settled in New York 1783, died there 17.8.1825,
buried in Greenwood Cemetery. [Comrie g/s]

MCLAREN, DUNCAN, born 1773, died in Glengarry, North
America, 1847. [Monzie g/s]

MCLAREN, HELEN, born 1797, died in Glengarry, North America,
7.3.1868. [Monzie g/s]

MCLAREN, PETER, born 1817, 'late of New York', died Main
Street, Barrhead, 6.11.1897. [Neilston g/s]

MCLAREN, PETER BAIN, born 1882, son of Robert McLaren and
Janet Stewart, died in Alberta 1.2.1909. [Kilmadock g/s]

MCLAUCHLAN, JAMES, born 1816, son of William McLauchlan and
Sarah McFarlane, died in Cleveland, Ohio, 12.11.1870.
[Buchlyvie g/s]

MCLAUCHLAN, ROBERT, born 1826, son of William McLauchlan
and Sarah McFarlane, died in Cleveland, Ohio, 1904.
[Buchlyvie g/s]

MCLAUCHLAN, WILLIAM, born 1793, died in Galt, Ontario,
11.3.1882. [Buchlyvie g/s]

MACLAUGHLIN, STEWART, born 1802, son of John MacLaughlin,
{1758-1824} a mason in Perth, and Margaret Kidd, {1771-1842},
died in New York 18.6.1855. [Perth, Greyfriars, g/s]

MCLEA, KENNETH, born 1800, a merchant in St Johns,
Newfoundland, died there 27.6.1862. [Greenock g/s]

MCLEAN, ALEXANDER, born 1827, died in Victoria, British
Columbia, 1888. [Anwoth g/s]

MCLEAN, CATHERINE, born 1809, daughter of Kenneth McLean
and Jean McVicar, died in St Johns, Newfoundland, 22.3.1866.
[Greenock g/s]

MCLEAN, DUNCAN, born 1749, a merchant in Petersburg, Virginia,
died there 10.4.1814, his wife Janet Milne born 1751 died in
Dundee 1.2.1835. [Dundee, Howff, g/s]

MCLEAN, JEANNIE, born 1868, daughter of Robert McLean and
Mary McCrindle, wife of Robert Shankland, died in Penkill,
Saskatoon, Canada, 12.2.1911. [Old Dailly g/s]

MCLEAN, NORMAN, born 1813 son of Charles McLean in
Gavinston, died in New York 12.2.1851. [Langton g/s]

MCLEAN, RODERICK, born 1845, son of John McLean {1796-1888} a farmer in Breakachie and Catherine Fraser {1809-1889}, died in America 1896. [Kilmorack g/s]

MCLEISH, JOHN, son of John McLeish and Jane Butchart {1789-1862}, settled in California. [Forfar g/s]

MCLEOD, ALEXANDER, Major of the North Carolina Highlanders, died 2.1797. [Old Dunvegan, Skye, g/s]

MCLEOD, CHARLES, born 1850, son of William McLeod and Jessie Black, died in West Hoboken, New Jersey, 4.7.1899. [Brechin Cathedral g/s]

MCLEOD, DONALD, son of Donald McLeod {died 1885} and Jane McDonald {died 1907}, died in New York 5.11.1912. [Golspie g/s]

MACLEOD, JAMES, son of Kenneth MacLeod and Jane Macleod, died in Conrad, USA, 20.7.1912. [Clyne g/s]

MCLEOD, JOHN, born 1805, son of James McLeod and Anne MacDonald, died in America 12.1861. [Creich g/s]

MCMASTER, Reverend ANGUS, son of Alexander McMaster {1729-1819} a farmer in Feorline and Flora McAlester {1760-1843}, a minister in Canada East. [Clachan g/s]

MCMASTER, ARCHIBALD, son of Alexander McMaster {1729-1819} a farmer in Feorline and Flora McAlester {1760-1843}, settled in Canada West. [Clachan g/s]

MCMASTER, Reverend JOHN, born 1802, son of Alexander McMaster {1729-1819} a farmer in Feorline and Flora McAlester {1760-1843}, '30 years in New Brunswick', died in Shedog, Bute, 6.4.1886. [Clachan g/s]

MCMILLAN, DAVID, born 1795, son of Robert McMillan {1757-1844}, died in Alabama 10.8.1842. [Monigaff g/s]

MCMILLAN, ELIZABETH, born 1854, wife of Robert Sproat, late in Lennox Plunton, died 12.4.1908, buried in Boise, Idaho. [Senwick g/s]

MCMILLAN, JOHN, born 1769 son of Robert McMillan {1749-1790} and Margaret Donaldson, died in Fayetteville, North Carolina, 7.10.1820. [Dumfries g/s]

MCMILLAN, WILLIAM, born 1850, son of Alexander McMillan and Helen Forsyth, died in Boston, Massachusetts, 1895. [Barrhill g/s]

MCMURDO, THOMAS, born 1811, son of Andrew McMurdo {1778-1866} and Ann Sharpe {1778-1872}, died in St Johns, Newfoundland, 1.4.1880. [Closeburn g/s]

MCMURTRIE, JAMES, born 1849, son of Adam McMurtrie and Margaret Wilson, died in Boston, USA, 1.9.1890. [Kirkmichael g/s]

MCNAB, DUNCAN, born in New York 30.12.1820, son of John McNab, died in New Scone 27.3.1854. [Muthill Innerpeffrey g/s]

MCNAB, HELEN, born in New York 30.10.1823, daughter of John McNab, died in New Scone 22.3.1845. [Muthill Innerpeffrey g/s]

MACNAB, JAMES, born 1817, son of John McNab {1757-1837} and Christine Buchanan {1786-1845}, died in Arthur township, Canada, 29.3.1872. [Callander, Buchanan, g/s]

MCNAB, JOHN, born 1782, "formerly in New York", died in New Scone 12.3.1858. [Muthill Innerpeffrey g/s]

MCNAB, PATRICK DAVID ROSS, born 1823, son of John McNab {1760-1852}, died in Chicago 31.12.1863. [Laggan g/s]

MACNAB, WILLIAM, born 1827, son of Alexander MacNab a wright in Rothesay and Janet Duncan, died in Virginia 19.2.1855. [Rothesay g/s]

MCNAUGHTON, Mrs ANN PLAYSTOWE, born 1808, wife of Lieutenant Colonel Duncan C. McNaughton, died in St Andrews, New Brunswick, 28.6.1893. [Craigs g/s]

MCNAUGHTON, CHRISTINE, born 1818, daughter of John McNaughton {1779-1853} a farmer, and Isabella Stewart {1784-1857}, wife of Reverend Duncan Cameron, died in Lucknow, Canada, 16.8.1885. [Logierait g/s]

MCNEIL, DUNCAN, born 1822, son of Malcolm McNeil {1797-1851} and Catherine ...{1797-1857}, died in Lake Erie 1851. [Greenock g/s]

MCNICOL, DANIEL, son of Daniel McNicol {1813-1873} and Mary Adam {1818-1882}, died in Richmond, Virginia, 14.6.1888. [Campsie g/s]

MACPHERSON, ALEXANDER, born 1816, son of Robert MacPherson in Bogside {1780-1850} and Elizabeth Holm {1786-1859}, died in Toronto 1872. [Inverkip g/s]

MCPHERSON, DUGALD, born 1834, son of Dugald McPherson {1784-1877} and Ann Sinclair {1793-1845}, died in Canada 23.1.1864. [St Modans, Ardchattan, g/s]

MCPHERSON, DUNCAN, son of John McPherson {died 30.8.1873} and Mary Tussell {died 11.6.1847}, settled in New York. [Kilmore Sleat g/s]

MCPHERSON, SAMUEL, born 1804, son of James McPherson {1766-1833} a farmer in Edinkille and Elspeth McPherson, died in Zaira, Upper Canada, 10.1839. [Kingussie g/s]

MCQUEEN, JAMES, born 1848, son of James McQueen and Helen McQueen, died in Pittston, Pennsylvania, 23.5.1872. [Anwoth g/s]

MCROBERT, JAMES, son of James McRobert {1775-1821} a farmer and Helen Beattie {1784-1830}, settled in America. [Strathdon g/s]

MCROBERT, JOHN, son of James McRobert {1775-1821} a farmer and Helen Beattie {1784-1830}, settled in America. [Strathdon g/s]

MCRUVIE, WILLIAM, son of Duncan McRuvie {1805-1856} and Agnes Scott {1800-1888}, died in Ballston Spa, USA, 2.4.1888. [Kilconquhar g/s]

MCTAGGART, ISAAC, born 1804, son of James McTaggart {1757-1832} and Mary Sproat {1761-1829}, died in Ottawa 18.12.1861. [Senwick g/s]

MABON, ADAM, born 1862, son of Alexander Mabon and Jane Barns, died in Bay City, Michigan, 24.7.1885. [Whitsome g/s]

MAIN, MARY, born 1830, daughter of John Main and Mary Houstoun, wife of John Watson, died in New York, 12.1.1861. [Borgue g/s]

MALCOLM, JOSIAH HAIG, born 1859, son of John Malcolm {1804-1864} and Janet Haig {1826-1882}, died in Brooklyn, New York, 9.11.1888. [Greenock g/s]

MALCOLM, ROBERT DOIG, born 1843, son of David Malcolm and Elspeth Doig, died in Belle Fourche, South Dakota, 1909. [Glamis g/s]

MALCOLM, WILLIAM, born 1818, son of Charles Malcolm {1789-1833} and Elizabeth Henry {1789-1871}, died in Newfoundland 23.9.1867. [Fordoun g/s]

MALLOCH, JAMES, born 1835, son of James Malloch and Janet
Shorthouse, died in Spencerport, America, 18.3.1860.
[Forgandenny g/s]

MANSON, WILLIAM, died in Charleston, South Carolina, 1836, his
wife Isabella Forbes born 1797, died in Auchterhouse 2.4.1867.
[Auchterhouse g/s]

MANTACH, Reverend WILLIAM, born 1792, son of John Mantach
{1743-1818} a farmer in Dundurcas, and Jane Hossack {1747-
1829}, died on Boaz Island, Bermuda, 18.12.1854.
[Dundurcas g/s]

MARR, GORDON, born 1848, died in Kaness, America, 11.3.1872.
[Dyce g/s]

MARSHALL, WILLIAM, son of William Marshall {died 1781} and
Christian Pilmore {1720-1751}, died in New Orleans
23.12.1803.[Dundee, Howff, g/s]

MARTIN, ALEXANDER, born 1808, died in Pittston, North America,
16.3.1871. [Carsphairn g/s]

MARTIN, ISABELLA, born 1807, daughter of James Martin {1734-
1806}, wife of Alexander Brown, died in Madison, Indiana,
3.9.1858. [Borgue g/s]

MARTIN, JAMES, born 1802, son of Thomas Martin and Nichola
Brown, died at Hangingrock, (USA?), 29.4.1874. [Borgue g/s]

MARTIN, JOHN GILLIES, born 1827, died in Paris, Canada West,
3.8.1854. [Lanark g/s]

MARTIN, SAMUEL, born 1813, son of Thomas Martin and Nichola
Brown, died in Laurenceburg, Indiana, 25.5.1867. [Borgue g/s]

MATHER, GEORGE, son of William Mather a merchant and Julia
Jane Brown, died in Brookly, USA, 16.12.1882. [Dunbar g/s]

MATHERS, SAMUEL, born 1828, son of Samuel Mathers {1774-
1828}, died in New Orleans 29.4.1872. [Dundee, Howff, g/s]

MATHESON, DUNCAN, son of Donald Matheson {died 1875} and
Isabella ... {died 1885}, settled in Colorado. [Gairloch g/s]

MATHESON, HECTOR, son of Donald Matheson {died 1875} and
Isabella ... {died 1885}, settled in Colorado. [Gairloch g/s]

MATHESON, KENNETH, son of Donald Matheson {died 1875} and
Isabella ... {died 1885}, settled in Colorado. [Gairloch g/s]

MATHESON, WILLIAM, born 1833, son of James Matheson and Jane
Ross, died in Stratford, Canada, 12.8.1857. [Dornoch g/s]

MATHIESON, Reverend D., in Montreal, son of George Mathieson
{1764-1845} and Janet Ewing {1764-1857}. [Campsie g/s]
MATTHEWSON, AGNES, born 1817, widow of William G. Dobie,
died in Kansas City, USA, 27.12.1893. [Dunfermline g/s]
MAXTON, ALEXANDER, born 1794, son of Reverend John Maxton,
died in Montreal, Quebec, 1830. [Alloa g/s]
MAXWELL, JOHN, born 1812, son of Alexander Maxwell and
Elizabeth Dutch, died in the Davis Strait 8.5.1837.
[Ferry Port on Craig g/s]
MAXWELL, JOHN, born 1848, son of John Maxwell and Marion
Mitchell, died in Toronto 14.5.1913. [Biggar g/s]
MAY, CHARLES, son of Benjamin May, Supervisor of Inland
Revenue, and Susannah Faith Bennett, died in Austin, Texas,
29.6.1882. [South Queensferry, Old, g/s]
MELDRUM, JOHN BALFOUR, born 1810, son of James Meldrum,
died in Paterson, New Jersey, 3.1883. [Leuchars g/s]
MELVILLE, ALEXANDER, son of Francis Melville {died 1890} and
Sarah Melville {died 1890}, died in Medford, Canada.
[Golspie g/s]
MELVILLE, JOHN, son of Francis Melville {died 1890} and Sarah
Melville {died 1890}, died in New York. Golspie g/s]
MELVILLE, WILLIAM, son of Alexander Melville of Hallfield, Fife,
{1784-1842} and Grace Babington {1779-1823}, died in Austin,
Texas, aged 25. [Dumfries g/s]
MELVILLE, WILLIAM, son of Francis Melville {died 1890} and
Sarah Melville {died 1890}, died in Toronto. [Golspie g/s]
MENNION, WALTER, born 1811, son of James Mennion and
Magdalene Craig, Government overseer in St George's,
Bermuda, died in Montreal 5.11.1858. [Ayton g/s]
MENZIES, THOMAS, son of James Menzies {died 1849} and Isabella
MacIntyre {died 1841}, settled in Peterborough, Canada.
[Comrie g/s]
MENZIES, WILLIAM, son of John Menzies {1788-1867} a farmer in
Lurcan, and Christiana Munro {1787-1863}, settled in
Wisconsin. [Weem g/s]
MERCHANT, JAMES, son of James Merchant {1783-1869} and
Elizabeth Guthrie {1773-1862}, settled in North America before
1869. [Arbuthnott g/s]

MERTON, AGNES, daughter of ..... Merton and Elisabeth Aitchison {1757-1832}, settled in Upper Canada. [Birgham g/s]

MERTON, ELISABETH, daughter of ..... Merton and Elisabeth Aitchison {1757-1832}, settled in Upper Canada. [Birgham g/s]

METHVEN, ALEXANDER, son of Thomas Methven and Mary Symmers, a surgeon, died in South Carolina, 1807. [St Andrews g/s]

MESSER, ALEXANDER, born 185-, son of Alexander Messer, {1810-1857}, an architect, and Jane Messer, died in Andover, Massachusetts, 1861. [Dingwall, St Clement's, g/s]

MESSER, ELIZABETH PEARSON, born 1852, daughter of Alexander Messer, {1810-1857}, an architect, and Jane Messer, died in Andover, Massachusetts, 18.. [Dingwall, St Clement's, g/s]

MESSER, JAMES, born 18.., son of Alexander Messer, {1810-1857}, an architect, and Jane Messer, died in Andover, Massachusetts, 189.. [Dingwall, St Clement's, g/s]

MESSER, Mrs JANE, wife of Alexander Messer {1810-1857}, died in Andover, Massachusetts, aged 76. [Dingwall, St Clement's, g/s]

MESSER, JOHN, son of Alexander Messer, {1810-1857} an architect, and Jane Messer, died in Halifax, USA, 1876. [Dingwall, St Clement's, g/s]

MICHIE, GEORGE, born in Corryhoul 25.10.1811, a merchant in Toronto, died in London 31.1.1860. [Strathdon g/s]

MIDDLETON, JANET, born 1762, wife of Peter Smith, died in Andover, Massachusetts, 8.1839. [Brechin Cathedral g/s]

MIDDLETON, JESSIE, born 22.12.1816, daughter of John Middleton and Jean Troup in Dundee, wife of Reverend Robert Sedgewick, died in Musquodoboit, Nova Scotia, 28.9.1878. [Perth, Greyfriars, g/s]

MILES, THOMAS, born 1832, son of Thomas Miles and Margaret Thomson, died at North Fork, American River, California, 24.5.1852. [St Andrews g/s]

MILL, DAVID, son of William Mill {1780-1859} and Margaret Dunn {1781-1875}, died in America 1840. [Westruther g/s]

MILLAR, ALEXANDER, born 1853, son of David Millar and Jean Aitken, died in Hinsdale, New Hampshire, 11.4.1925. [Stirling g/s]

MILLER, DAVID, born 1808, son of David Miller and Isabella
Gilchrist, died in the St Lawrence River, Canada, 12.5.1827.
[Dundee, Howff, g/s]

MILLER, FRANCIS, son of John Miller {1777-1841} and Helen Ross
{1780-1861}, settled in Mexico. [Lanark g/s]

MILLER, GEORGE, son of George Miller and Janet Morrison, died in
Savannah 28.9.1839. [Tulliallan g/s]

MILLER, JAMES F., son of Thomas Miller {died 1809} a shipmaster
in Dundee and Elizabeth Gardiner {died 1818}, settled in New
York. [Dundee, Howff, g/s]

MILLER, JOHN, son of James Miller {1730-1818} a glover, died in
Philadelphia 11.5.1836. [Canongate g/s]

MILLER, PETER, born 1796, died in Montreal 1.8.1832. [Cullen g/s]

MILLER, ROBERT, born 1817, son of David Miller {1776-1824} a
brewer, and Isabella Gilchrist {1767-1849}, died in New Orleans
6.12.1850. [Dundee, Howff, g/s]

MILLER, STOCKS, son of Walter Miller and Sarah Stocks, died in
Moorcroft, Wyoming, 8.1890. [Logie, Fife, g/s]

MILLER, WILLIAM FORRESTER HARDY, born 1833, died in
Portland, Maine, 26.4.1898. [Old Calton g/s]

MILLIGAN, ROBERT, son of Thomas Milligan {1785-1857} a
plumber in Dumfries and Alison Wight Anderson, died in New
York aged 37. [Dumfries g/s]

MILLS, ROBERT, born 1844, son of Robert Mills and Agnes
Jamieson, died in Toronto 7.1.1884. [Brechin Cathedral g/s]

MILNE, ALEXANDER, son of Robert Milne {1832-1904} in Hillhead,
Caskieben, and Isabella Henderson {1834-1905}, settled in
Bixbys, Dakota. [Dyce g/s]

MILNE, DAVID, born 1792, late farmer in Kinkell, died 28.6.1887,
husband of Ann Scott, born 1798, died 2.5.1865, parents of Ann,
born 1823 - died 7.9.1865, Jessie, born 1837 - died 25.1.1872,
and William, born 1817- died 18.11.1883, - "All interred in
America." [Fordoun g/s]

MILNE, DAVID, son of Robert Milne {1832-1904} in Hillhead,
Caskieben, and Isabella Henderson {1834-1905}, settled in
Ogden, Utah. [Dyce g/s]

MILNE, GEORGE, born 1834, son of John Milne and Isabella
Lindsay, died in Orient, USA, 14.2.1904. [Kirriemuir g/s]

MILNE, JAMES, born 1848, son of John Milne {1821-1899} and
Margaret Paterson {1823-1850}, died in Texas 29.6.1897.
[Bellie Tynet g/s]

MILNE, JANE MENMUIR, born 1856, daughter of William Milne, a
gardener in Stitchill, died in East Milton, Massachussetts,
17.8.1888. [Stitchill g/s]

MILNE, JOHN ALEXANDER RADCLIFFE, born 16.11.1860, son of
Andrew Jamieson Milne and Annie Lewis Hodgson, died in New
Orleans 24.10.1896. [Fyvie g/s]

MITCHELL, HANNAH GRACE, born 1844, daughter of John
Mitchell {1821-1911} and Mary Mitchell {1822-1907}, died
17.3.1850 in Newfoundland. [Rothesay g/s]

MITCHELL, JOHN, born 1792, died in Kingston, Upper Canada,
6.10.1823. [Keig g/s]

MITCHELL, JOHN EDWARD, born 1847, son of John Mitchell
{1821-1911} and Mary Mitchell {1822-1907}, died 14.12.1849 in
Newfoundland. [Rothesay g/s]

MITCHELL, JOHN, born 1850, son of John Mitchell {1821-1911} and
Mary Mitchell {1822-1907}, died 28.10.1850 in Newfoundland.
[Rothesay g/s]

MITCHELL, MAGDALENE, born 1838, daughter of James Mitchell
{1800-1872} and Elizabeth Thomson {1800-1843}, died in
Barony, New Brunswick, 25.1.1872. [Larbert g/s]

MITCHELL, THOMAS, son of Robert Mitchell and Margaret
Carmichael, died in Montreal 10.8.1848. [St Andrews g/s]

MITCHELSON, DAVID, born in Kirriemuir, Angus, 26.1.1732, 'late
of New York', died at Fyfe Place, Leith Walk, Edinburgh,
24.10.1802. [Canongate g/s]

MOFFAT, ALEXANDER, born 1803 son of Andrew Moffat {1768-
1845} a baker in Duns, died in Charleston, South Carolina,
17.9.1819. [Duns g/s]

MOFFAT, ANDREW, born 1794 son of Andrew Moffat {1768-1845}
a baker in Duns, died on Sullivan's Island, South Carolina,
22.8.1849. [Duns g/s]

MOFFAT, GEORGE, born 1800, son of Andrew Moffat, died in
Charleston, South Carolina, 21.8.1844. [Duns g/s]

MOIR, CHARLES, born 1842, son of Adam Moir {1809-1869} and Ann Crichton {1807-1891}, died in Erie, Pennsylvania, 31.10.1882. [Dundee, Eastern Necropolis, g/s]

MONCRIEFF, FRANCIS EDWARD, born 1858, son of George Moncrieff and Angela Birch, died in Toronto 7.1.1884. [Perth, Wellshill, g/s]

MONTGOMERIE, WILLIAM, born 1760, son of Matthew Montgomerie and Ellicot Menzies, died in America 1781. [Paisley Abbey g/s]

MOODIE, JAMES, born 1829, son of James Moodie and Mary Pearson, died in Quincy, Massachusetts, 3.4.1900. [Monigaff g/s]

MOODIE, JOHN, born 1834, son of James Moodie and Mary Pearson, died in Hamilton, Canada, 19.10.1902. [Monigaff g/s]

MORGAN, WILLIAM, born 1863, son of Alexander Morgan {1811-1880} and Helen Malcolm {1816-1906}, died at Stone Mountain, Georgia, 20.9.1890. [Monymusk g/s]

MORRISON, DAVID, born 1802, died in America 10.8.1855. [St Cuthbert's, Edinburgh, g/s]

MORRISON, ROBERT, Pictou, Nova Scotia, a sailor on the Genoa, drowned off Rattray Head, Aberdeenshire, 12.4.1863. [Rattray g/s]

MORTIMER, SAMUEL, born 1835, son of Samuel Mortimer and Lillias Glenday, died in USA 15.7.1859. [Glamis g/s]

MORTON, AGNES, daughter of ... Morton and Elizabeth Aitchison {1757-1832}, settled in Upper Canada. [Birgham g/s]

MORTON, ALEXANDER, born 1823, son of Robert Morton and Sarah Reid, died in Lyons, America, 30.5.1862. [Carluke g/s]

MORTON, J.A.Thomson, son of Robert Morton and Elizabeth Amderson, died in Bermuda 7.5.1861. [Strathmiglo g/s]

MOYES, WILLIAM, died in Alameda County, California, 13.5.1879. [Dundee, Howff, g/s]

MUIR, ISABELLA, born 1825, daughter of Thomas Muir and Isabella McKinlay, widow of Alexander Nairn, died in Montreal 23.12.1907. [Rothesay g/s]

MUIR, ROBERT LIVINGSTONE, born 1824, died in St John's, Newfoundland, 6.6.1865. [Greenock g/s]

MUIR, WILLIAM, born 1868, son of Thomas Muir and Grace Alexander Prentice, died 1913, buried in New York.
[Lanark g/s]

MUIR, WILLIAM CHARLES, son of Charles B. Muir and Robina Frances Hunter, died in Montreal 2.2.1860. [Canongate g/s]

MUNDIE, WILLIAM, a gardener in Toronto, son of William Mundie, crofter in Cortes, {1771-1855} and Grisel Murison {1770-1829}.
[Rathen g/s]

MUNNOCH, PETER, son of Peter Munnoch and Margaret Forfar, settled in California by 1898. [Polmont g/s]

MUNROE, ALEXANDER H., born 1845, son of James Munroe {1817-1867} and Mary Hamilton {1820-1848}, died in Los Angeles, California, 27.12.1881. [Crosbie g/s]

MUNRO, ALEXANDER ROSE, born in Invernald 20.5.1835, son of George Munro and Christine Mackay, died in Montreal 9.8.1869. [Creich g/s]

MUNRO, ANDREW, born 1823, son of Andrew Munro and Isabella Urquhart, died in San Francisco, California, 20.6.1852.
[Avoch g/s]

MUNRO, CATHERINE, daughter of Robert Munro and Margaret ......, settled in Charleston, South Carolina, before 1807.
[Crail g/s]

MUNRO, CHARLES, born 1861, son of Alexander Munro {1816-1889} and Margaret Jaffrey {1823-1889}, died in Vancouver, British Columbia, 4.9.1892. [Tyrie g/s]

MUNRO, DONALD, son of John Munro {1755-1827} and Florence McSporran {1755-1820}, a farmer in Canda, County York, America. [Cladh Nam Paitean, Kintyre, g/s]

MUNRO, DONALD, son of David Munro {died 1890} and Margaret MacDonald {died 1911}, died in Helena, Montana, 12.11.1886.
[Kincardine Ardgay g/s]

MUNRO, Reverend HARRY, born 1730, late Rector of St Peter's, Albany, New York, died in Edinburgh 30.5.1801.
[Edinburgh, St Cuthbert's, g/s]

MUNRO, JOHN, born 1819, son of Alexander Munro miller in Kilmachalmaig, died in New York 11.5.1864.
[Kincardine Ardgay g/s]

MUNRO, WILLIAM, born 1864, son of Hugh Munro and Jesie
Simpson, died in Guttenberg, New Jersey, 15.10.1904.
[St Clement's, Aberdeen, g/s]

MURCHESON, JOHN, son of John Murcheson {1779-1867} and Eliza
Mackenzie {1786-1877}, settled in Sommerville, Union County,
Oregon. [Kishorn g/s]

MURDOCH, DAVID RITCHIE, born 1859, son of John Murdoch and
Flora Ritchie, died in Montreal 12.11.1894.
[Edinburgh, St Cuthbert's, g/s]

MURDOCH, MARY, born 1848, daughter of Andrew Murdoch and
Mary Cumming, wife of James Carson, died on Clark's Island,
USA, 23.3.1909. [Colvend g/s]

MURPHY, WILLIAM, son of Jane Cram {1808-1877}, settled in
Hamilton, Ontario. [Crosbie g/s]

MURRAY, ADAM COWAN, born 1845, son of Robert Murray and
Mary Cowan, died in Petersburg, Virginia, 25.3.1865.
[Crossmichael g/s]

MURRAY, ALEXANDER, born 1814, son of Hector Murray and
Catherine Brown, died in New Orleans 1854.
[Pollockshaws, Kirk Lane, g/s]

MURRAY, ANN, born 1830, died in Woburn, Massachusetts,
27.7.1893. [Dornoch g/s]

MURRAY, ANNIE, died in Dover, Ontario, 27.2.1904. [Tyrie g/s]

MURRAY, CHARLES, born 1812, son of Reverend Andrew Murray
{1754-1844} and Janet Mackie, died in Louisiana 1853.
[Auchterarder g/s]

MURRAY, DONALD, born 1849, son of Donald Murray and Jane
Munro, died in Quilchena, British Columbia, 22.8.1897.
[Dornoch g/s]

MURRAY, HUGH, son of David Murray {1788-1844} and Janet
McDonald {1789-1873}, settled in Ontario. [Loth g/s]

MURRAY, JAMES WOLFE, born in Louisbourg, Canada, 1759, son
of Alexander Murray, died 1836. [Edinburgh, Greyfriars, g/s]

MURRAY, JOHN, son of John Murray {1764-1820} a merchant and
Janet Shaw {1779-1859}, died in Eweke, USA, aged 72.
[South Leith g/s]

MURRAY, MARY, born 1845, daughter of Donald Murray and
Hugina Morrison, died in America 20.6.1891. [Durness g/s]

MURRAY, WILLIAM, born 1821, son of William Murray and
Christian Murray, died in Ohio 22.9.1854. [Fetteresso g/s]

MURRAY, WILLIAM, born 1855, son of Walter Murray amd Elspet
MacKintosh, died in Vancouver 8.1927. [Dornoch g/s]

MURRAY, WILLIAM, a merchant in Halifax, New Brunswick, son of
Robert Murray and Margaret Gray, "perished in the ship City of
Boston" which left Halifax 28.1.1870. [Dornoch g/s]

MYLES, ELIZA CRAIG, born 1848, daughter of Robert Myles and
Helen Cellars, wife of John Honeyman, died in Emerson, Mills
County, Iowa, 15.5.1874. [Cupar g/s]

M....., ROBERT, born 1798, son of J. M....... and Christian Garrow,
died in South Carolina 1.11.1819. [Fetteresso g/s]

NAIRN, JAMES, born 1800, son of John Nairn and Isabel Lawson,
died in Quebec 4.10.1840. [Arbroath Abbey g/s]

NEIL, WILLIAM, born 1823, son of James Neil and Margaret
Montgomerie, died in Chatham, Canada West, 12.6.1861.
[Riccarton g/s]

NEILSON, JOHN, born in Dornal 17.7.1776, son of William Neilson
and Isabel Brown, Member of HM Legislative Council of
Canada, died at Cape Rouge, Quebec, 1.2.1848. [Balmaghie g/s]

NEILSON, JOSEPH, son of William Neilson {1803-1898} and Mary
Finlayson {1811-1898}, died in America 5.11.1871.
[Dunblane g/s]

NEILSON, MARGARET, born 1800, second wife of James
McLauchlan, died in Galt, Ontario, 12.3.1822. [Buchlyvie g/s]

NEILSON, MARY, born 1824, daughter of John Neilson and Janet
Herries, wife of James Scott, died in Lynden, Cattaraugus City,
North America, 29.1.1869. [Kirkgunzeon g/s]

NEILSON, SAMUEL, born 5.8.1770 in Dornel, son of William
Neilson and Isabel Brown, died in Quebec 12.1.1793. [Balmaghie
g/s]

NEILSON, SAMUEL, born 1863, son of Walter Neilson and Anne
Caven, died in Ashton, Illinois, 3.4.1895. [Kirkgunzeon g/s]

NEILSON, WILLIAM, born 22.9.1772, son of William Neilson, "an
advocate for civil and religious liberty in America", died
8.5.1857. [Balmaghie g/s]

NICHOLL, JOHN, born 1828, son of William Nicholl {1802-1890} a
shepherd, died in America 1852. [Teviothead g/s]

NICHOLSON, AGNES REID, daughter of William Nicholson and
Maria Lamb, died in Washington, USA, 27.11.1881.
[Edinburgh, St Cuthbert's, g/s]

NICHOLSON, JAMES, born 1782, died in Miramachi 4.9.1848.
[Dumfries g/s]

NICOLL, DAVID, born 3.5.1847, son of James and Jane Nicoll,
shipmaster, died in Port Townsend, Washington, 14.1.1897.
[Monifieth g/s]

NICOLSON, ALEXANDER, born 1845, son of Angus Nicolson and
Euphan Mackenzie, died in Chicago 8.5.1872. [Osmigarry g/s]

NICOLSON, DAVID, born 1868, son of David Nicolson and Mary
Dunnet, died in Kelso, British Columbia, 14.8.1900.
[Canisbay g/s]

NICOLSON, ROBERT, son of William Nicolson {1695-1779} a
burgess tailor of Dunbar and Margaret Spiers {1692-1779}, a
merchant in Williamsburg, Virginia. [Dunbar g/s]

NOBLE, FRANCES ELIZA, born in Williamstown, Massachusetts,
5.12.1821, wife of Arthur F. Stoddard, died 25.10.1885.
[Port Glasgow g/s]

NOBLE, ROBERT, son of Robert Noble {died 1793} and Janet Grieve
{1750-1836}, died in Halifax, Nova Scotia, 1846. [Peebles g/s]

OFFICER, JAMES, born 1845, died in Walkerville, Canada
4.11.1915, buried in Windsor, Canada. [Montrose, Rosehill, g/s]

OLIPHANT, WILLIAM, born 1843, son of Walter Oliphant, died in
Canada 23.11.1884. [Edinburgh, St Cuthbert's, g/s]

ORR, JAMES RAMSAY, born 1807, a merchant in Montreal, died
16.3.1852. [Stirling g/s]

ORR, JOHN, born 1813, died in Montreal 20.4.1856.
[Edinburgh, New Calton, g/s]

OSBURNE, ROBERT, son of Janet Wilson Osburne {1796-1858}, a
merchant in Chicago. [Dunbarton g/s]

OUGHTERSON, ARTHUR DEANE, born 1829, son of John
Oughterson and Janet Robertson, died in Concordia, USA,
21.3.1882. [Helensburgh g/s]

PALMER, WILLIAM, born 1795, son of William Palmer and
Margaret Neilson, died in North America 10.1826.
[Balmaghie g/s]

PATON, DAVID, born 1840, son of George Paton and Ann Pearson, died in Canada 7.10.1911. [Dundee, Trottick, g/s]

PATON, DAVID, born 1862, son of Thomas Paton, died in Texas 21.2.1886. [Balgonie g/s]

PATTERSON, ADAM, born 1814, son of Andrew Paterson and Christine Paterson, died in Paris, Upper Canada, 21.3.1841. [Edinburgh, New Calton, g/s]

PATTERSON, ARCHIBALD, born 1800, in Pictou, Nova Scotia, died in Glasgow 25.9.1821. [Paisley Gaelic g/s]

PATTERSON, DOROTHY JESSIE, born 14.1.1890 in Broadview, Canada, daughter of Robert Patterson and Jessie Maria Bevis, died in Salford 14.6.1907. [Gargunnock g/s]

PATERSON, ELIZABETH, born 1780, daughter of John Paterson {1747-1831} and Jean Tweedie {1742-1821}, died in Long Grove, Iowa, 2.12.1866. [West Linton g/s]

PATERSON, JESSIE, born 1830, wife of James Rossie, died in Topeka, Kansas, 24.2.1905. [Dunning g/s]

PATERSON, NEIL WILLIAM, born 1779, son of John Paterson {1747-1831} and Jean Tweedie {1742-1821}, died in Montreal 21.7.1834. [West Linton g/s]

PATERSON, R.B., son of Robert Paterson {1811-1897} and Margaret Low {1812-1851}, settled in St John, Canada. [Portmoak g/s]

PATTON, HENRY WILLIAM, born 1836, son of William Patton, died in Benares, Canada West, 19.5.1855. [Fossoway g/s]

PAUL, ALEXANDER, born in Banff 3.5.1848, died in Lake Huron 7.1870. [Banff g/s]

PAUL, MARGARET, born 1826, daughter of John Paul and Margaret Henderson, died in Quincy, Gadsden County, Florida, 7.9.1872. [Halkirk g/s]

PEACOCK, THOMAS, born 1841, son of Thomas Peacock MD, died 6.2.1903 in Hoprig, Emmet County, Iowa. [Edinburgh, Liberton, g/s]

PEDDIE, JOAN, born 1844, daughter of William Peddie and Agnes Imrie, died in La Cros, Wisconsin, 13.7.1916. [Perth, Greyfriars, g/s]

PEDEN, Reverend ROBERT, born 1815, son of John Peden and Janet Morton, died in Hamilton, Canada West, 5.10.1858. [Kilmarnock, St Andrew's, g/s]

PETRIE, JOHN, son of Henry Petrie {1752-1833} and Helen Douglas
{1775-1859}, died in Meadville, USA, 1833.
[Dundee, St Andrew's, g/s]

PETTICRUE, JOHN, born 1795, son of William Petticrue {1768-1828}
feuar in Halrig, died in America 12.7.1824.
[Tarbolton g/s]

PIRIE, J.T., a merchant in New York, son of Allan Pirie {1796-1874}.
[Errol g/s]

PITTENDRIGH, ELIZABETH HELEN, born 1863, daughter of
George Pittendrigh and Margaret Masson, wife of Robert Marr,
died in Canada 4.6.1901. [Udny g/s]

PORTEOUS, CHRISTINA, born 1856, daughter of John Porteous
{1824-1902}, died in New York 30.5.1901, buried in Yantic
Cemetery, Norwich, Connecticut. [West Linton g/s]

PORTEOUS, JOHN, born 1824, husband of Annie Gray, died in
Norwich, USA, 21.11.1902. [West Linton g/s]

PORTEOUS, WILLIAM, born in Napan, Miramachi, New Brunswick,
17.10.1837, minister in Bellahoustoun, Glasgow, died in Inellan
28.11.1864. [Dunoon g/s]

POW, DAVID, born 1856, son of James Pow and Margaret Cargill,
died in Eden, USA, 4.5.1890. [Arbroath Abbey g/s]

PRATT, ALISON, born 1787, widow of Ninian Lockhart, died in
Philadelphia 10.6.1878. [Abbotshall, Kirkcaldy, g/s]

PRENTICE, JANE DENT, daughter of James Prentice and Grace
Black, died in Brooklyn 27.3.1903. [Cambusnethan g/s]

PRENTICE, THOMAS, born 1798, son of Archibald Prentice in
Cleghorn Mill, Lanark, died in Philadelphia 28.6.1821.
[Covington g/s]

PRINGLE, JOHN, born 1836, son of John Pringle, jeweller in Perth,
and Janet Cameron, died in New York 8.6.1869. [Perth,
Greyfriars, g/s]

PROCTOR, ALLAN, born 1853, son of Richard Proctor and Helen
Low, died in South Chicago, USA, 13.10.1908.
[Arbroath Abbey g/s]

PULLAR, THOMAS, born 1833, died in New Britain, Connecticut,
3.3.1901. [Little Dunkeld g/s]

PURDIE, ALEXANDER, born 1767, son of Alexander Purdie and
Janet Scott, died in Syracuse, North America, 9.10.1834.
[Thankerton g/s]

PURVIS, BURRIDGE, of Glassmount, Fife, born 1776, a merchant,
died in Greenock 10.7.1816, on return from South Carolina,
husband of Mary Brown. [Greenock, Inverkip St., g/s]

PURVIS, JOHN, born 1823, son of John Purvis and Elizabeth Findlay,
died in Upper Canada 28.3.1864. [Arbroath Abbey g/s]

RAE, ANN BELL, born 1844, daughter of Thomas Rae and Janet Bell,
died in Dow City, Iowa, 20.6.1888. [Kettle g/s]

RAE, CECILIA, died in Sydenham, Owen Sound, Canada West,
1.6.185... [Swinton g/s]

RAE, ISOBELLA, born 1855, daughter of Thomas Rae and Janet Bell,
died in Dow City, Iowa, 3.1888. [Kettle g/s]

RAE, JESSIE, daughter of James Rae, died in California 16.1.1901.
[Preston, Berwickshire, g/s]

RAE, THOMAS, born 1846, son of Thomas Rae and Marion B.
Ballantyne, settled in New York, died in Ingleside, New Canaan,
Connecticut, 8.11.1909. [Coulter g/s]

RAMSAY, ALEXANDER, Lieutenant of the Royal Artillery, third son
of Captain Ramsay of the Royal Navy, died in New Orleans
1.1.1815. [Inveresk g/s]

RANDALL, ELIZABETH WIRT, born 1828, daughter of Judge
Thomas Randall in Tallahassie, Florida, granddaughter of
William Wirt, Attorney General of the United States 1817-1829,
wife of James Clunas, died at Cawdor Place, Nairn, 3.10.1863.
[Wardlaw g/s]

REDDIE, JOHN OATTS, born 1859, son of David Reddie {1821-
1898} and Jane Spittall {1819-1890}, died in Prince Rupert,
British Columbia, 28.8.1912. [Stirling, Holy Rude, g/s]

REID, ADAM, born 1801, son of Peter Reid {1760-1808}, a merchant
in Baltimore, died 1886. [Glenbuchat g/s]

REID, ALEXANDER, born 1795, son of John Reid and Elizabeth
Mill, died in North America 12.1819. [Benholm g/s]

REID, ALEXANDER, died in Washington 15.4.18.. aged 49.
[Dundee, Old Mains, g/s]

REID, HELEN, born in Edinburgh 21.4.1811, daughter of Sir James John Reid and Mary Threshie, widow of William Keir, advocate, died in Brantford, Ontario, 16.10.1884.
[Edinburgh, Greyfriars, g/s]

REID, JAMES, born in New Deer, 1760, son of William Reid and Jean Hall, Chief Justice of the Court of Queen's Bench in Montreal, died 19.1.1848. [New Deer g/s]

REID, JAMES, born 1875, son of James Reid {1841-1923}, died in Acme, Alberta, 7.10.1911. [Avoch g/s]

REID, JOHN, born 1826, son of Hugh Reid and Elizabeth Wylie, died in Utica, North America, 13.8.1852, buried in Ottawa.
[Kilmarnock g/s]

REID, PETER, born 1760, "sometime of Baltimore", died 10.8.1808.
[Glenbuchat g/s]

REID, ROBERT G., son of William Reid {1818-1867} and Catherine Gillespie {1811-1909}, died in Montreal 1908.
[Coupar Angus g/s]

RIACH, JOHN, born 1826, son of John Riach {1778-1875} a farmer, and Margaret Anderson {1792-1875}, died in Toronto 5.2.1855.
[Rothes g/s]

RICHARDSON, WILLIAM, born 1775, emigrated to Upper Canada 1833, died there 3.3.1840. [Borthwick, Roberton, g/s]

RIDDICK, JOHN, son of John Riddick {1820-1867}, died in America 1872. [Southwick g/s]

RITCHIE, JAMES ANDREW, born 31.8.1844, son of Reverend William Ritchie {1805-1895} and Margaret Brown {1819-1898}, died in Chicago 11.7.1879. [Longforgan g/s]

ROBB, ANDREW, born 1837, son of Bryce Robb and Mary Ann Gehan, died in New York 29.12.1887. [Balmaghie g/s]

ROBB, WILLIAM, born 1790, son of George Robb {1748-1828} a farmer in Quothquan and Helen Girdwood {1749-1834}, died in Roanoke, North Carolina, 16.10.1819. [Skirling g/s]

ROBERTSON, ADAM, born 1784, a painter, died in Charleston, South Carolina, 9.12.1838. [Arbroath g/s]

ROBERTSON, ANN, born 1813, wife of John Burnett, died in Chicago, Illinois, 9.12.1854. [Tyrie g/s]

ROBERTSON, DANIEL, born 1861, died in Montreal 8.1.1892.
[Kilmarnock, St Andrew's, g/s]

ROBERTSON, DAVID, born 1821, son of George Robertson {1793-1865} a hosier, and Maria Esther Ireland {1797-1844}, died in Sacramento City, California, 29.6.1850. [Dundee, Eastern Necropolis, g/s]

ROBERTSON, DAVID, born 1834, son of Robert Robertson and Janet Kennedy, died in Chicago 3.3.1871. [Logerait g/s]

ROBERTSON, DUNCAN, born 1808, son of .... Robertson and Jane Inches, died in New York 17.10.1839. [Dundee, Howff, g/s]

ROBERTSON, ELIZABETH, born 1830, daughter of William Robertson, {1802-1894}, tenant in Cuttlebrae, and Elizabeth Sutherland {1799-1851}, wife of ... Sutherland, died in New York, 16.1.1861. [Bellie g/s]

ROBERTSON, HOPE FLEMING, born 1825, daughter of John Robertson and Susan Fleming, died in St Louis, USA, 28.11.1883. [Logierait g/s]

ROBERTSON, ISABELLA, born 1828, daughter of William Robertson and Elizabeth Sutherland, died in Grimsby, Canada West, 19.11.1869. [Bellie g/s]

ROBERTSON, JAMES GUTHRIE LAKE, born 1812, son of Charles Robertson {1784-1833} and Isabella Guthrie {1788-1861}, a merchant in Nashville, USA, died in Newport on Tay 1.2.1881. [Dundee, Western, g/s]

ROBERTSON, JAMES, born 1825, son of John Robertson {1790-1849} and Janet Small {1793-1859}, died in Arthur, America, 18.9.1883. [Rattray g/s]

ROBERTSON, JOHN, son of John Robertson {1765-1837} a farmer and Margaret Robertson {1776-1848}, Senator of the Dominion of Canada. [Dowally g/s]

ROBERTSON, JOHN, born in USA 1838, died 29.9.1860. [Edinburgh, Dalry, g/s]

ROBERTSON, JOHN, born 1823, son of David Robertson and Helen Malloch, died in Florida 1878. [Perth, Greyfriars, g/s]

ROBERTSON, JOSEPH, born 1857, son of David Robertson and Louisa Hood, died in Chicago 10.3.1882. [Montrose, Episcopal, g/s]

ROBERTSON, MALCOLM, born 1796, son of Donald Robertson {1755-1809} and Mary McColl {died 1804}, died in Canada West 1818. [Isle Munda, Ballahulish, g/s]

ROBERTSON, MARIA, born 1829, daughter of George Robertson and Mary Esther Ireland, drowned off Newfoundland 27.9.1854. [Dundee, Eastern Necropolis, g/s]

ROBERTSON, MARJORIE, born 1820, daughter of Andrew Robertson brewer in Longforgan, wife of R. Christie, died in Melbourne, Canada, 19.12.1866. [Longforgan g/s]

ROBERTSON, RODERICK, son of Donald Robertson {1841-1882} and Christine Fraser {1843-1879}, settled in Chicago. [Dornoch g/s]

ROBERTSON, SAMUEL, New York, drowned in the wreck of the brig Petrel of Stockton off Boarhills, Fife, 30.11.1839. [Boarhills g/s]

ROBERTSON, WILLIAM, born 1803, son of David Robertson and Helen Malloch, died in Chicago 3.1877. [Perth, Greyfriars, g/s]

ROBISON, WILLIAM, born 1763, son of ..... Robison and Mary Clark, died in Bergen Neck, New Jersey, 24.1.1849. [Balmaghie g/s]

ROGER, CHARLES, born 1854, son of Robert Roger and Agnes Brown, died in Leadville, Colorado, 24.2.1901. [Liff g/s]

ROGERS, HENRY DARWIN, born in Philadelphia 1809, geologist, Professor at Dickenson College, USA, then Professor in Glasgow University, died in Glasgow 29.5.1866. [Edinburgh, Dean, g/s]

ROMANES, ROBERT ROSE, born in Elmsley, Canada, 11.1838. son of Reverend George Romanes and Isabella Cair, died in Kingston, Canada, 7.3.1849. [Edinburgh, Greyfriars, g/s]

ROME, JANET, born 1822, faughter of George Roe and Agnes Paterson MacRae, wife of Robert Rankin, died in Moulton, Canada, 31.7.1876. [Kilmarnock, St Andrews, g/s]

RONALDSON, JAMES, son of William Ronaldson of Gorgie {1737-1817} and Marion Cleghorn {1734-1825}, settled in Philadelphia. [Colinton g/s]

RONALDSON, JANET, daughter of William Ronaldson of Gorgie {1737-1817} and Marion Cleghorn {1734-1825}, died in Philadelphia before 1840. [Colinton g/s]

RONALDSON, JOHN, son of William Ronaldson of Gorgie {1737-1817} and Marion Cleghorn {1734-1825}, died in Norfolk, Virginia. [Colinton g/s]

RONALDSON, JOHN, born 1807, son of Archibald Donaldson {1767-1832}, died in Philadelphia 2.1.1842. [South Leith g/s]

RONALDSON, RICHARD, son of William Ronaldson of Gorgie {1737-1817} and Marion Campbell {1734-1825}, settled in Philadelphia. [Colinton g/s]

ROSS, ALEXANDER, born 1756, son of Alexander Ross {1712-1785} and Catherine Rutherford {1711-1785}, died in New York 26.12.1805. [Kinnoull g/s]

ROSS, CATHERINE FORBES, born 1828, daughter of George Ross {1778-1847} and Grace Ross {1785-1833}, died in Renfrew, Ontario, 2.12.1892. [Dingwall, St Clement's, g/s]

ROSS, CHARLES THOMSON, born 1884, died in Toronto 15.9.1910. [Caputh g/s]

ROSS, DAVID, born 1788, son of John Ross a cooper in Dundee and Jean Lindsay, {1749-1821}, died in New York 29.1.1818. [Dundee, Howff, g/s]

ROSS, GEORGE CLARK, born 25.10.1798, died in Brompton, Canada East, 1.11.1852. [Crossmichael g/s]

ROSS, GEORGE, son of Robert Ross {1757-1827} an innkeeper in Dornoch and Mary Ann Mackay {1756-1830}, a merchant in Quebec. [Dornoch g/s]

ROSS, JAMES, son of George Ross {died 1850} and Anne Fullerton {died 1876}, died in Catalina, Newfoundland, 6.9.1864. [Brechin Cathedral g/s]

ROSS, JOHN, born 1832, son of Duncan Ross and Margaret Maclay, died in Carbondale, Pennsylvania, 14.2.1885. [Dornoch g/s]

ROSS, PATRICK DAVID, born 1823, son of Reverend Thomas Ross in Kilmanivaig, died in Chicago 31.12.1863. [Laggan g/s]

ROSS, THOMAS, born 1786, son of John Ross {1740-1855} a carpenter in Dingwall, died in Toronto 20.8.1856. [Dingwall, St Clement's, g/s]

ROSS, Mrs THOMAS, born 1795, died in Quebec 4.12.1856. [Carluke g/s]

ROSS, WILLIAM, son of Alexander Ross {1746-1806} and Henrietta Ross {1763-1812}, a merchant in Toronto. [Lairg g/s]

ROSS, WILLIAM, born 1861, son of Hugh Ross and Mary Forbes, died in Hawaii 1.4.1895. [Kincardine Ardgay g/s]

ROSS, WILLIAM, born 1828, died in Montreal 14.10.1899.
[Dunbarton g/s]

ROY, ANTHONY, born 1871, son of John Roy and Janet McCreath,
died in Pocatello, Idaho, 8.1.1901. [Straiton g/s]

ROY, PETER, born 1812, son of John Roy {1767-1847} and Mary
Davidson {1788-1821}, died in Pittsfield, USA, 24.12.1840.
[Logie Old, g/s]

RUSSELL, ELIZABETH, born 1822, died in San Francisco,
California, 8.8.1888. [Mertoun g/s]

RUSSELL, HENRY, son of Henry Russell and Agnes Beaton, died in
Baltimore 2.1846. [Kettle g/s]

RUSSEL, JAMES, born 1815, son of William Russel, 'late of
California' died 1904. [Kinnedar, Moray, g/s]

RUSSELL, JAMES, born 1868, son of James Russell and Barbara
Scott, died in San Francisco 22.11.1897. [Cupar g/s]

RUTHERFORD, GEORGE, born 1816, son of Thomas Rutherford
{1773-1835} and Margaret Hay {1776-1837}, died in New York
13.7.1835. [Westruther g/s]

RUXTON, JOHN, born 1842, son of James Ruxton and Mary Low,
died in America 12.4.1895. [Arbroath Abbey g/s]

RYRIE, ALEXANDER, born 1865, son of James Ryrie and Charlotte
Swanson, died in San Francisco 1.12.1900. [Olrig g/s]

SANG, DAVID, born 1800, husband of Helen Brodie, died in New
York 15.10.1842. [St Andrews g/s]

SAVILE, MARY, born 1806, wife of John Anderson a merchant in
Mexico, died 3.10.1844. [Edinburgh, Old Calton, g/s]

SCHOLLAY, HELLEN PARIS, born 1856, daughter of David
Schollay and Jane Simpson, died in Denver, Colorado,
17.10.1899. [Arbroath Abbey g/s]

SCHOOLAR, JAMES, born 1823, son of John Schoolar, died in
California 11.4.1883. [Hutton g/s]

SCOTT, ALEXANDER, born 1716, son of Reverend John Scott, a
clergyman in Virginia, died 1737. [Dipple g/s]

SCOTT, ALEXANDER, born 1738, Captain of the 35th Regiment,
died in Montreal 4.4.1778. [Montrose g/s]

SCOTT or ALEXANDER, BETHIA, born 1842, daughter of William
Scott {1804-1873} and Bethia Brown {1806-1878}, died in
Streetsville, Ontario, 6.1889. [Slamannan g/s]

SCOTT, DAVID, born 1870, son of William Scott and Jane Earl, died
in New York 17.3.1895. [Old Kilpatrick g/s]

SCOTT, GRACE, born 1799, wife of James Forrest, died in New York
3.3.1877. [Bathgate, Kirkton, g/s]

SCOTT, JAMES, born 1715, son of Reverend John Scott of Loch and
Marjory Stewart, a clergyman in Virginia. [Dipple g/s]

SCOTT, JAMES, son of Hugh Scott {1760-1815} and Marion
McCallan {1768-1820}, settled in Montreal. [Ballantrae g/s]

SCOTT, JAMES, born 1844, a saddler, died in Calgary, Canada,
10.3.1921. [Lanark g/s]

SCOTT, JAMES HARPER, born 1857, died in Origaba, Mexico,
20.3.1888. [Greenlaw g/s]

SCOTT, JEAN, born 1833, wife of William Taylor, died in San
Francisco 7.6.1891. [Montrose, Episcopal, g/s]

SCOTT, JOAN, born 1.6.1848, daughter of Henry Scott and Elizabeth
Edgely, wife of Tom Allen, died in Aurora, Illinois.
[Chirnside g/s]

SCOTT, JOHN, son of John Scott {1750-1813} a schoolmaster and
Jane French {1750-1816}, died in America. [Monimail g/s]

SCOTT, JOHN R., born 1853, son of David Scott and Margaret
Ritchie, died in Chicago 29.8.1889. [Girvan g/s]

SCOTT, ROBERT, born 1814, a grocer, died in Forrest, Canada West,
25.1.1883. [Lanark g/s]

SCOTT, THOMAS, born 1746, eldest son of Reverend Alexander
Scott and Euphan Henderson, Chief Justice of Upper Canada,
died 1824. [Meigle g/s]

SCOTT, THOMAS, born in Ashkirk 1756, an Episcopal minister in
North America for 25 years, returned to Scotland in 1812, died
in Edinburgh 28.8.1828. [Ashkirk g/s]

SEATON, JOHN, born 1828, son of James Seaton and Margaret
Fairweather, died in Perry, Canada, 5.5.1877.
[Arbroath Abbey g/s]

SHAND, GEORGE, born in Arbroath 1820, died in New York 1887.
[Arbroath Abbey g/s]

SHARP, JAMES, born 1790, son of William Sharp and Isabella
Kinnear, a tanner, died in New Orleans 13.8.1829. [Dundee,
Howff, g/s]

SHAW, JOHN, son of Robert Shaw {1799-1866} and Ann McEwing {1801-1882}, a merchant in Forrest, Ontario. [Houston g/s]

SHAW, MATTHEW LYMBURNER, born 1755, settled in Canada, died in Edinburgh 17.2.1842. [Kilmarnock, Laigh, g/s]

SHEPHERD, DAVID, son of William Shepherd {1792-1832}, settled in New Orleans, Louisiana, before 1847. [Dunfermline g/s]

SHEPHERS, JOHN MUNRO, born 1853, son of George Shepherd and Isabel Middleton, died in Missuala, Montana, 18.9.1902. [Montrose, Rosehill, g/s]

SIBBALD, MARY W., born 1825, daughter of David Sibbald and Anne Sibbald, died in California 8.11.1853. [Dundee, St Peter's, g/s]

SIM, DANIEL, born 1858, son of John Sim and Anne Kennedy, died in Des Moines, USA, 12.7.1914. [Little Dunkeld g/s]

SIM, GEORGE, born 1850, son of William Sim {1821-1893} and Mary Stewart {1824-1908}, died in San Francisco 1906. [Braemar g/s]

SIM, PETER, born 1852, son of William Sim {1821-1893} and Mary Stewart {1824-1908}, died in Montreal 1928. [Braemar g/s]

SIM, THOMAS, born 1807, died in Halifax, North America, 1851. [Birnie g/s]

SIME, JOHN, son of Thomas Sime {1806-1883} and Isabella Nicoll {1801-1869}, died in America aged 21. [Dundee, St Peter's, g/s]

SIME, LEWIS, born 1848, son of Alexander Sime {1796-1873} and Margaret Donaldson {1811-1882}, died in St Thomas, Canada, 15.3.1871. [McAllen, Knockando, g/s]

SIMSON, ANN, born 1764, widow of the late William Lyon of Halifax, Nova Scotia, died 8.1850. [Rothesay g/s]

SIMPSON, JOHN, born in Marnoch 1747, a merchant in Quebec. [Marnoch g/s]

SIMPSON, JOHN, son of James Simpson {1770-1852} and Christine Whyte {1777-1841}, died in New Orleans 16.10.1843. [Kirkcaldy g/s]

SIMPSON, ROBERT, born 1817, son of James Simpson {1785-1856} and Helen Williamson {1780-1869}, died in Boston, Massachusetts, 10.6.1841. [Cramond g/s]

SINCLAIR, CATHERINE, born 1810, daughter of Donald Sinclair {1781-1867} and Catherine Thompson {1788-1865}, wife of George Robin, died in Wisconsin 1851.

[St Modans, Ardchattan, g/s]

SINCLAIR, MARGARET, daughter of Hector Sinclair {died 1853} and Anne McMishie {died 1851}, wife of John Robertson, died in Toronto 23.8.1865. [Old Petty g/s]

SINCLAIR, PETER, son of Peter Sinclair {1808-1871}, settled in Prince Edward Island. [Glen Daruel g/s]

SKINNER, ISABELLA SMITH, daughter of William Skinner and Isabella Davidson, died in Florida 1.12.1886. [Kirkcaldy g/s]

SKINNER, WILLIAM, born 10.4.1839, died in St Louis, USA, 23.8.1869. [Abbotshall, Kirkcaldy, g/s]

SLOSS, DUNCAN, son of Andrew Sloss {1782-1847}, died in California aged 45. [Colmonell g/s]

SLOSS, JOAN, born 1825, wife of David McCosh, died in Hannibal, America, 12.7.1849. [Colmonell g/s]

SMALL, ANDREW, son of Andrew Small {1766-1794} and Anne Wright {1765-1822}, settled in Washington, DC. [Liff g/s]

SMEATON, THOMAS WRIGHT, born 15.5.1859, son of Reverend John Smeaton and Mary Drummond Wright, died in Canada 17.8.1909. [Auchterarder g/s]

SMITH, ALEXANDER, born 1807, son of Alexander Smith and Elizabeth Rae, died in New York 19.4.1852. [New Machar g/s]

SMITH, ALEXANDER, born 1813, son of Alexander Smith shoemaker in Aberdeen and Isabella Main {1779-1827}, died in New Orleans 10.3.1848. [Banchory Tiernan g/s]

SMITH, ANDREW, born 1790, late a surgeon in Montreal, died in Smithfield, 21.4.1824. [Riccarton g/s]

SMITH, CECILIA, born in Cambusnethan 1.1822, wife of William Bell, died in Elderslie, Ontario, 4.1.11882. [Carbarns, Cambusnethan, g/s]

SMITH, DAVID, born 1796, son of Robert Smith and Janet Henderson, a merchant in New Orleans, died in Perth 27.12.1882. [Logie, Fife, g/s]

SMITH, DAVID, born 1828, son of James Smith and Martha Sime, died in New York 13.1.1861. [Arbirlot g/s]

SMITH, DONALD, born 1858, son of Robert Smith and Elizabeth Robertson, died in Cincinatti 25.8.1883. [Canisbay g/s]

SCOTTISH-AMERICAN GRAVESTONES

SMITH, HARRIET DUDLEY, born in Jackson, Mississippi, 8.2.1844,
wife of George T. Ure {1847-1930}, died in Bonnybridge
3.1.1889. [Larbert g/s]

SMITH, HENEAGE HORSLEY, born 1843, son of James Smith
{1794-1843} and Helen Small {1810-1900}, died in Garnet,
Alabama, 14.10.1884. [Dundee, Constitution Road, g/s]

SMITH, Reverend JAMES, DD, born in Glasgow 11.5.1798, '40 years
a minister in USA', appointed as US Consul in Dundee by
Abraham Lincoln whose pastor he had been and where he died
3.7.1871. [Glasgow, Calton, g/s]

SMITH, JAMES, born 24.8.1816 son of Alexander Smith a shoemaker
in Old Machar, Aberdeen, and Isabella Main {1779-1827},
settled in Buffalo, New York, before 1827.
[Banchory-Tiernan g/s]

SMITH, JAMES, born 1828, son of James Smith and Martha Sim, died
in New York 13.1.1861. [Arbirlot g/s]

SMITH, JESSIE KERR, born 1844, daughter of William Smith and
Janet Kerr, wife of A.A.Anderson, died in Hamilton, Ontario,
26.7.1882. [Arbroath Abbey g/s]

SMITH, JOHN, son of Reverend Ebenezer Smith {1757-1816} and
Janet Carruthers {1758-1831}, a merchant in New York. [Borgue
g/s]

SMITH, JOHN, son of Peter Smith {1762-1810} and Janet Middleton
{1762-1839}, settled in Andover, Massachusetts. [Brechin
Cathedral g/s]

SMITH, JOHN ELDER, son of John Smith and Ann Hutton Elder, died
in New York 28.4.1887. [St Monance g/s]

SMITH, Reverend JOHN MALCOLM, Queen's College, Kingston,
Canada, died 3.8.1856. [Edinburgh, Grange, g/s]

SMITH, KENNEDY, born 1824, son of Robert Smith and Elizabeth
Brown, died in Berbeth, Maine, 19.5.1870. [Old Dailly g/s]

SMITH, MARIA, born 1843, daughter of Alexander Smith and
Barbara Guthrie, died in San Francisco 12.9.1882.
[Arbroath g/s]

SMITH, PETER, son of Peter Smith {1762-1810} and Janet Middleton
{1762-1839}, settled in Amdover, Massachusetts. [Brechin
Cathedral g/s]

89

SMITH, ROBERT, born 14.8.1804, son of James Smith {1777-1863} a merchant in Greenock and Ann Farm {1777-1851}, a merchant in Quebec, died 16.5.1842. [Johnstone g/s]

SMITH, ROBERT LESLIE, born 1863, son of John J. Smith and Isabella Walker, died in Providence, Rhode Island, 21.2.1895. [St Andrews g/s]

SMITH, Reverend THOMAS, born 1746, son of James Smith a blacksmith in Edingham, minister of the Seceder Congregation in Huntington, Pennsylvania, died 24.8.1825. [Colvend g/s]

SMITH, WILLIAM, born 1808, son of Walter Smith and Elizabeth Goodlet, died in New York 31.10.1865. [St Vigean's g/s]

SNODDY, ADAM, Governor of York Factory, Hudson Bay, died in Stromness 20.12.1834. [Canisbay g/s]

SOMERVILLE, ELIZA, daughter of John Somerville, died 11.7.1863, buried in Springdale Cemetery, Peoria, Illinois. [Airth g/s]

SOMERVILLE, GEORGE BROWN, son of Robert Banks Somerville {died 1907} and Helen R. Graham {died 1915}, died in Philadelphia 22.2.1904. [St Ninian's g/s]

SOMERVILLE, WILLIAM, son of John Somerville {1754-1811} a farmer in Bonnington and Janet Somerville {1753-1808}, died in Clear Creeks County, Indiana, 7.9.1821. [Peebles g/s]

SPEED, ANN, born 1864, daughter of John Speed and Isabella Elder, died at Traer Toma, Iowa, 5.10.1882. [Longforgan g/s]

SPENCE, JAMES, born 1792, son of Thomas Spence and Catherine Colville, died on passage to America 14.2.1819. [Dundee, Howff, g/s]

SPOTTISWOODE, ROBERT, sixth son of William Spottiswoode of Glenfernate {1747-1830} and Janet Mitchell {1770-1826}, died in America 1855. [Kirkmichael g/s]

SPROAT, ALEXANDER, born 1740, son of John Sproat, died in Ohio 1825. [Senwick g/s]

SPROAT, GILBERT MALCOLM, born 1834, died in Victoria, British Colimbia, 4.6.1913. [Senwick g/s]

SPROAT, JOHN, born 1720, son of John Sproat and Elizabeth Johnston, died in Pennsylvania 1800. [Senwick g/s]

SPROAT, ROBERT, born 1837, son of Hugh Sproat and Mary MacMillan, died in Emmith, Isaho, 26.3.1925. [Senwick g/s]

STANFORD, PETER, born 1805, died in Connecticut 16.12.1858.

[Monigaff g/s]

STARK, JOHN, son of William Stark {1730-1806} and Margaret Hervey {1737-1806}, settled in Canada. [Westruther g/s]

STARK, JOHN C., born 1812, son of ... Stark and Emma Brown, died in Philadelphia 29.12.1838. [St Cuthbert's, Edinburgh, g/s]

STEDMAN, ROBERT, soldier of C Company, the Maine Infantry Volunteers, died during the US Civil War 1861-1865. [Old Calton, Edinburgh, g/s]

STEEL, WALTER, born 1842, died in Maine 18.7.1921. [Dalbeattie g/s]

STEPHEN, ALEXANDER, son of James Stephen {died 1854} a baker, and Ann Booth {died 1841}, settled in America before 1877. [Rothes g/s]

STEPHEN, JOHN, born 1840, son of James Stephen and Jane Craig, died in Alameda, California, 13.7.1892. [Dunnottar g/s]

STEVENSON, Reverend ARCHIBALD, son of William Stevenson {1797-1872} and Isabella ... {1802-1882}, died in St Rennie, Napierville County, Quebec, 8.10.1907. [Stirling, Holy Rude, g/s]

STEVENSON, DAVID, born 1876, son of James Stevenson and Jane Blair, died in Thermopolis, Wyoming, 18.9.1909. [Kirkoswald g/s]

STEVENSON, MARGARET, wife of John Brebner, died 25.12.1898, buried in Woodlawn, New York. [Perth, Wellshill, g/s]

STEVENSON, MARY, born 8.10.1809, daughter of Hugh Stevenson and Janet Nelson, died in America 1892. [St Ninian's g/s]

STEWART, ALEXANDER, son of James Stewart {1800-1872} and Annie McLaren {1808-1894}, died in Port Lavaco, America, 1897. [Blair Atholl g/s]

STEWART, ALEXANDER, born 1818, son of Walter Stewart and Mary Hill, died in Colorado Springs, USA, 17.4.1884. [Forfar g/s]

STEWART, ALEXANDER, born 1832, son of Alexander Stewart {1778-1831} and Margaret Allan {1799-1838}, died in Chicago 9.4.1864. [Glasgow, Bridgeton, g/s]

STEWART, ANDREW DAVID, born 3.9.1813, son of James Alston Stewart {1763-1833} and Charlotte Stewart {1780-1837}, died in Missouri 17.5.1848. [Moulin g/s]

STEWART, DANIEL, born 1803, "sometime of Cayuka, Hamilton, Canada," died 31.10.1883. [Dunblane g/s]

STEWART, DUNCAN, son of Duncan Stewart {1794-1867} and Helen Woodrow {1797-1880}, a merchant in Detroit. [Fintry g/s]

STEWART, JAMES, born 13.11.1785, a merchant in Greenock and in Newfoundland, died 11.11.1837. [Greenock g/s]

STEWART, JAMES AFFLECK, son of Robert Stewart and Ann Stewart, Captain of the 11th Hussars, died in Brantford, Canada West, 15.5.1867. [Forgan g/s]

STEWART, JAMES, born 1815, son of Thomas Stewart and Mary Gemmell, died in Otanbee, Canada, 7.9.1883. [Fenwick g/s]

STEWART, JAMES, born 1843, son of David Stewart in Spittalfield {1812-1872} and Margaret Duncan {1816-1885}, died in Saginaw, USA, 17.6.1891. [Caputh g/s]

STEWART, JOHN, son of Donald Stewart and Janet Grant, a Hudson Bay Company employee prior to 1830, died in Morayshire 14.1.1847. [Abernethy g/s]

STEWART, JOHN, born 1802, died in Lucesco, Pennsylvania, 19.12.1894. [Whithorn g/s]

STEWART, JOHN MCGREGOR, born 1824, son of Roger Stewart, {1744-1822} a merchant, and Jean .... {1758-1822}, died in New Orleans 2.1858. [Greenock, Inverkip Street, g/s]

STEWART, KATE, daughter of Fergus Stewart and Mary Graham Sinclair, died in Denver, USA, 14.11.1886.
[Kilnonver, Argyll, g/s]

STEWART, ROGER, born 1822, son of Roger Stewart,{1744-1822} a merchant, and Jean ... {1758-1822}, died in Springhill, Mobile, Alabama, 25.5.1858. [Greenock, Inverkip St., g/s]

STIRTON, GRACE, born 1787, widow of Peter Slater, died in Canada West, 29.12.1878. [Gartmore g/s]

STIVEN, ANDREW, born 1822, son of William Stiven and Margaret Air, died in Goderich, Ontario, 19.3.1883. [Arbroath Abbey g/s]

STIVEN, PETER, born 1831, son of William Stiven and Agnes Scott, died in Detroit, Michigan, 1858. [Strathcathro g/s]

STOBIE, GEORGE, son of Thomas Stobie {1752-1841} and Margaret Condie {1774-1852}, died in Ebobicok, Western Canada, 15.10.1855. [Portmoak g/s]

STODDARD, ARTHUR FRANCIS, of Broadfields, born in
Northampton, Massachusetts, 30.11.1810, died 3.6.1882.
[Port Glasgow g/s]

STODART, ADAM, born 1783, died in New York 27.7.1872.
[Covington g/s]

STODART, ARCHIBALD, born 1846, son of Archibald Stodart and
Agnes Robertson, died in Buena Park, California, 24.12.1913.
[Covington g/s]

STODART, DAVID RIDDLE, born 1832, died on Staten Island, New
York, 14.11.1893. [Edinburgh, New Calton, g/s]

STODART, JOHN, born 1782, son of James Stodart {1757-1829} and
Agnes Thomson {1757-1839}, died in Uttica, USA, 15.12.1834.
[Covington g/s]

STODDART, JOHN. son of James Stoddart {1784-1868} a shepherd in
Newark and Isabella Richardson {1790-1886}, died at Cloves
Branch Junction, New York, aged 50 years. [Selkirk g/s]

STODART, MARION, born 1791, died in Louisville, America,
9.7.1848. [Covingston g/s]

STOTT, ELIZABETH, born 1853, wife of F. Gaynor, died in San
Francisco, 1.12.1889. [Edinburgh, St Cuthbert's, g/s]

STRACHAN, DAVID, born 1859, died 1925, buried in Boston,
Massachusetts. [Brechin Cathedral g/s]

STRACHAN, GEORGE, born 1842, son of William Strachan and
Lizzie McEwan, died in Valley Falls, Rhode Island, 17.3.1916.
[Brechin Cathedral g/s]

STRANG, THOMAS, died in America 18.., second wife Ann
Crawford and their daughter Elizabeth both died in America
18... [Pollockshaws, Kirk Lane, g/s]

STRATTON, GEORGE, born 1837, son of John Stratton and Margaret
Wyness, a papermaker, died in Paterson, New Jersey, 6.9.1894.
[Dyce g/s]

STRONG, ALEXANDER, born 1859, son of Alexander Strong {1824-
1899} in Blairgowrie, died in Chicago 22.7.1893. [Bendochy g/s]

STRONG, PETER, born 1821, son of James Strong and Grace
Ramsay, died in Iowa 19.2.1899. [Bendochy g/s]

STUART, JOHN WILLIAM, born 1861, son of Robert Stuart {1833-
1910} and Helen Grant {1840-1924}, died in Chicago 5.8.1912.
[Aberlour g/s]

SCOTTISH-AMERICAN GRAVESTONES

STUART, MARY, daughter of Robert Stuart {1833-1910} and Helen
Grant {1840-1924}, died in Chicago 11.1915. [Aberlour g/s]
STUART, PETER, son of Robert Stuart {1833-1910} and Helen Grant
{1840-1924}, died in Chicago 5.1914. [Aberlour g/s]
STURROCK, DAVID, born 1825, son of David Sturrock and Betsy
Miller, died in St John's, Newfoundland, 17.11.1854. [Arbroath
Abbey g/s]
SUTHERLAND, ANN, born 1780, wife of John Miller, died in
Toronto, America, (sic), 17.4.1847. [Lanark g/s]
SUTHERLAND, CATHERINE, born 1861, daughter of Donald
Sutherland and Elspeth Mackay, died in Zora, Canada, 7.5.1898.
[Dornoch g/s]
SUTHERLAND, CHRISTINA, born 1857, daughter of James
Sutherland and Margaret Cumming, wife of James Sutherland,
died 17.3.1893, buried in Denver. [Ballachy g/s]
SUTHERLAND, CHRISTINE, daughter of John Sutherland {1790-
1875} and Christine Mann {1820-1868}, died in Embro, Canada.
[Dornoch g/s]
SUTHERLAND, DONALD, son of James Sutherland {1792-1862} and
Catherine Sutherland {1792-1870}, settled in Woodstock, Canada
West, before 1871. [Golspie g/s]
SUTHERLAND, DONALD, born 1851, son of William Sutherland and
Janet Sutherland, died in America 30.1.1893. [Canisby g/s]
SUTHERLAND, ELIZABETH, born 1816, daughter of Robert
Sutherland and Elizabeth Sutherland, drowned in Nova Scotia
11.1832. [Latheron Old g/s]
SUTHERLAND, HELEN, born 1875, died in British Columbia
27.2.1895. [Latheron Old g/s]
SUTHERLAND, HUGH, born 1821, son of Boyce Sutherland and
Barbara McKay, died in Canada 26.4.1904. [Durness g/s]
SUTHERLAND, JAMES, born 1840, son of William Sutherland and
Jane Sutherland, died in New York 17.9.1864. [Rogart g/s]
SUTHERLAND, JOHN, born 1834, died in Kinlough, Ontario,
6.5.1914. [Navidale g/s]
SUTHERLAND, JOHN MACKAY, born 1852, died in Ailsa, New
Jersey, 14.11.1879. [Edinburgh, St Cuthbert's, g/s]
SUTHERLAND, WILLIAM, born 1847, died in Ailsa, New Jersey,
28.6.1895. [Edinburgh, St Cuthbert's, g/s]

SUTHERLAND, ..., daughter of James Sutherland {1811-1889} and Helen Ross {1813-1851}, wife of Alexander Matheson, settled in West Zotta, Canada. [Dornoch g/s]

SWAN, JOHN, born 1870, died in San Francisco, 10.5.1887. [Dalbeattie g/s]

SWANSTON, ROBERT, born 1802, son of John Swanston and Janet Williamson, died in America 11.7.1878. [Carmichael g/s]

SWEET, Reverend WALLACE GRAHAM, born in Langside, died in Montreal aged 45. [Cathcart g/s]

SYMINGTON, JAMES, born 1800, son of James Symington and Mary Thomson, an innkeeper, died in Montreal 25.7.1877. [Lanark g/s]

SYMON, JANE, born 15.7.1830, wife of John Forbes, died in Toronto 24.12.1909. [Strathdon g/s]

TAIT, PETER, born 1781, a tenant farmer in Horndean, husband of Agnes Hogarth {1779-1817}, died in Chicago 18.5.1836. [Whitsome g/s]

TASKER, PATRICK, born 1843, a merchant in St Johns, Newfoundland, died 11.1880. [Greenock g/s]

TAWSE, ALEXANDER MCLAUGHLAN, born 1832, son of George Tawse {1794-1872} and Catherine ...{1800-1881}, died in Toronto 22.3.1873. [Dundee, Eastern Necropolis, g/s]

TAYLOR, DAVID, born 1790, son of John Taylor and Jean Reid, died in Welham, America, 17.2.1861. [Fordoun g/s]

TAYLOR, ELIZABETH, born 1775, daughter of Robert Taylor {1770-1831} a merchant and Jean Taylor {1770-1846}, wife of John Melville, died in Wetheredville, USA, 20.10.1866. [Barrhead, Arthurlie, g/s]

TAYLOR, HUGH, son of Donald Taylor, died in Nevada 10.1890. [Dornoch g/s]

TAYLOR, JAMES, son of William Taylor {1745-1812} a farmer and Helen Walker {1759-1847}, a merchant in Savannah, Georgia. [Fordoun g/s]

TAYLOR, JOHN, son of Andrew Taylor {1788-1870} and Jane Milne {1801-1882}, a merchant in St Louis, USA. [Fordoun g/s]

TAYLOR, WILLIAM, born in Dundee 1790, son of William Taylor, to America with his parents in 1803, died in New York 23.3.1811, buried in Dundee 27.3.1813. [Dundee, Howff, g/s]

TENCH, CAROLINE MARGARETTA, born 1815, wife of John Laing in Upper Canada, died in Edinburgh 7.4.1836. [Restalrig g/s]

THAIN, THOMAS, born 1779, son of John Thain {1739-1816}, settled in Montreal, died 1832. [Forgue g/s]

THOMPSON, ALEXANDER, born 1734, son of James Thompson {1714-1770} an Excise accountant, and Agnes Smith {1717-1745}, settled in Savannah, Georgia, a Loyalist, died in Edinburgh 1798. [Canongate g/s]

THOMSON, ALFRED, born 1876, son of John Thomson, died in Mexico City, 14.9.1914. [Kilmarnock g/s]

THOMSON, Reverend JAMES, born 1724, son of George Thomson a merchant in Falkirk, married Jane Chapman 1763, emigrated to America 1785, 'labored some time in the Lord's work in America', died in Dundee 17.11.1791. [Dundee, Howff, g/s]

THOMSON, JAMES, born 1783, son of ..... Thomson and Barbara Dewar {1745-1835}, died in Charleston, South Carolina, 17.9.1802. [Forgandenny g/s]

THOMSON, JAMES, born 1804, son of James Thomson in Kilbank and Ann Scott {1783-1815}, died in Quebec 1836. [Lesmahagow g/s]

THOMSON, JAMES, born 1813, son of Thomas Thomson {1783-1857} and Jane Bell {1789-1838}, died in America 22.9.1861. [New Scone g/s]

THOMSON, JAMES, born 1815, son of John Thomson {1774-1845} a merchant in Stonehaven and Elspet Lyon {1781-1837}, died in Beaufort, South Carolina, 9.4.1843. [Fetteresso g/s]

THOMSON, JAMES, born 1828, son of Andrew Thomson and Ann White, drowned in the St Lawrence River 26.9.1856. [Methilhill g/s]

THOMSON, JANE, wife of W. Manson, died in New York 2.4.1893. [Edinburgh, Old Calton, g/s]

THOMSON, JESSIE, born 1841, daughter of John Thomson and Jane Thomson, died 7.10.1913, buried in Toronto. [Arbroath Abbey g/s]

THOMSON, JOHN, born 1736, died in North Carolina 7.1790. [Colvend g/s]

THOMPSON, JOHN, born 1742, son of William Thompson and Agnes
Aitken, died in North Carolina 7.1796. [Colvend g/s]
THOMSON, JOHN, born 1813, son of Thomas Thomson and Jane
bell, died in America 22.9.1861. [New Scone g/s]
THOMSON, JOHN, born 1814, son of Peter Thomson {1766-1849}
and Catherine Thomson {1784-1833}, a merchant in America,
died 12.4.1853. [Milnathort g/s]
THOMSON, JOHN, son of Duncan Thomson {1810-1867} and Mary
Mun {1818-1891}, died in Brantford, Canada, 24.5.1886.
[Alexandria g/s]
THOMSON, MALCOLM, born 5.9.1850, son of Neale Thomson of
Camphill {1807-1857}, drowned in the Natasquhan River,
Labrador, 1.7.1873. [Cathcart g/s]
THOMSON, PETER, born 1770, son of Robert Thomson {1717-1783}
and Agnes Lewers {1741-1811}, died in Philadelphia 16.7.1795.
[Colvend g/s]
THOMSON, PETER, born 1824, son of Peter Thomson and Catherine
Thomson, a merchant in San Francisco, died in Oakland,
California, 9.8.1901. [Milnathort g/s]
THOMSON, ROBERT, born 1814, son of J. Thomson in Kilbank and
Ann Scott {1783-1815}, died in New York 1840.
[Lesmahagow g/s]
THOMSON, STEWART, son of Duncan Thomson {1810-1867} and
Mary Munn {1818-1891}, died in Brantford, Canada, 4.1.1910.
[Alexandria g/s]
THOMSON, WILLIAM, born 1810, son of Andrew Thomson and
Janet Paterson, died in Montreal 27.5.1842. [Ashkirk g/s]
THORBURN, JOHN, born 1777, son of David Thorburn {1742-1826}
tenant farmer in Roadhead, Quothquan, died 5.3.1866, buried in
Mount Royal Cemetery, Montreal. [Carnwath g/s]
TIDYMAN, Sir PHILIP, born 1772 in Charleston, South Carolina,
died in Aberdeen 11.6.1850. [Old Aberdeen g/s]
TOCHER, JOHN, born 1871, son of William Tocher {1841-1909} and
Margaret Barclay {1844-1920}, died in California 1888.
[Tyrie g/s]
TODD, ALEXANDER, son of Alexander Todd {1774-1851} and
Martha Spiers {1776-1846}, settled in New Orleans, Louisiana.
[Houston g/s]

TODD, DAVID, born 1820, son of David Todd and Mary Wyllie, died in St Louis, USA, 15.1.1888. [Inverkeilor g/s]

TOSH, DAVID, son of James Tosh {1824-1873} and Mary Ann McNab {1830-1898}, died on Edisto Island, South Carolina, 23.3.1894. [Dundee, Western, g/s]

TOSHACH, JAMES, born 1827, son of James Toshach and Isabel Stewart, died in Canada 1887. [Dron g/s]

TOUGH, CHARLES, son of Charles Tough in Auchendoir {1769-1853} and Margaret Paul {1777-1865}, settled in Ontario. [Auchendoir g/s]

TOUGH, DAVID, born 1860, son of David Tough and Ann Williams, died in New Mexico 9.5.1891. [Dundee, Eastern Necropolis, g/s]

TROKES, MAXWELL, born 1781, a merchant in Virginia, died in Glasgow 4.12.1852. [Glasgow, Blackfriars, g/s]

TROTTER, ISABELLA, born 1827, daughter of Robert Trotter and Catherine McDougal, died in America 11.5.1859. [Chirnside g/s]

TURNBULL, JAMES, born 1853, son of Adam Turnbull and Ann Tripney, died at Barton on the Sound, USA, 9.12.1881. [Muiravonside g/s]

TURNBULL, JAMES, born 1836, son of George Turnbull and Rachel Clyde, died in America 14.11.1898. [Borthwick g/s]

TURNBULL, JANET, born 1839, daughter of Thomas Turnbull and Isabella Black, wife of John Ballentyne, died in Boston, Massachusetts, 19.8.1907. [Galashiels g/s]

TURNBULL, JOHN, born 1865, son of John Turnbull and Agnes Irvine, died in Newark, USA, 14.8.1899. [Stirling g/s]

TURNBULL, WILLIAM, born 1821, son of William Turnbull of Forthbank {1767-1851} and Jean Colquhoun {1781-1852}, died in Newmarket, Upper Canada, 10.3.1847. [St Ninian's, New, g/s]

TURNER, COLL JOHN, born 1827, died in Brooklyn, USA, 29.12.1897, buried in Greenwood Cemetery. [Luss g/s]

TURNER, JOHN, born 4.2.1814, Lieutenant of the 56th Regiment, died in Lower Canada 17.4.1841. [Inveraray g/s]

TWEED, ALEXANDER, son of William Tweed {1683-1760} and Jean Jaffray, a planter in South Carolina. [Banff g/s]

URE, JOHN, born 1815, died in Oakland, California, 12.5.1897. [Dunbarton g/s]

URQUHART, GEORGE, born 1871, son of Donald Urquhart and
Annie Ross, died in Montreal 21.3.1912.
[Kincardine Ardgay g/s]
URQUHART, JAMES, born 1796, a plasterer, died in Philadelphia
5.11.1833. [Banchory Devenick g/s]
VANCE, AGNES, born 1868, daughter of David Vance {1828-1887},
died in Canada 15.11.1887. [Whithorn g/s]
VANCE, JANET, daughter of John Vance {1800-1867} and Janet
Aitken {1813-1890}, wife of John Bryce, died in Astoria,
Oregon, 8.4.1878. [Stirling, Holy Rude, g/s]
VEITCH, JAMES, son of David Veitch and Emelia Wight, a surgeon,
died at Moose Factory, Canada, 1832. [Musselburgh g/s]
WAID, RICHARD, born in Philadelphia 20.7.1768, son of ..Waid and
Susan Waid, died 28.10.1787. [Dundee, Howff, g/s]
WAIT, JOHN, born 1826, son of Robert Wait and Mary Hislop, died
on James Island, Charleston, South Carolina, 16.6.1862.
[Ladykirk g/s]
WALKER, ANN, born 1829, daughter of James Walker and Jessie
Spink, wife of William Leitch, died in Hamilton, Ontario,
18.3.1899. [Arbroath Abbey g/s]
WALKER, ARCHIBALD, son of Robert Walker {1735-1805} and
Herries Gray, died in Virginia 5.2.1805. [Dumfries g/s]
WALKER, GEORGE, born 1854, son of John Walker, an innkeeper,
and Jane Smith, died in Buffalo, USA, 1.11.1888.
[Monymusk g/s]
WALKER, JAMES, born 1845, son of Adam Walker and Ann ..., died
in New Orleans 15.3.1874. [Luss g/s]
WALKER, JAMES GRAY, born 1851, son of William Walker {1814-
1893} and Margaret Gray {1815-1878}, died in San Francisco
17.8.1891. [Edinburgh, Grange, g/s]
WALKER, JOHN, son of George Walker {1809-1861} and Janet
Ogilvie {1810-1870}, drowned in River Stiken, British
Columbia, 29.8.1862. [Dundee, Western, g/s]
WALKER, MARGARET, daughter of John Walker, died in New York
8.1849. [St Andrews g/s]
WALKER, MARGARET, born 1836, daughter of James Walker and
Jessie Spink, wife of William Hendrie, died in Hamilton,
Ontario, 15.7.1873. [Arbroath Abbey g/s]

WALKER, Mrs MARGARET, widow of John Walker, died in New York 8.1875. [St Andrews g/s]

WALKER, PARTHINIA, daughter of John Walker, and widow of John Carmichael, died in New York 1855. [St Andrews g/s]

WALKER, THOMAS, son of Robert Walker {died 1854} and Isabella Kerr {died 1860}, died in Troy, USA, 9.2.1881. [Earlston g/s]

WALKER, THOMAS, born 1852, son of John Walker and Mary Williamson, died in Jackson, USA, 24.5.1893. [Clyne Kirkton g/s]

WALKER, WILLIAM, born 1810, son of Andrew Walker and Isobel Landale, died in Williamsburgh, New York, 9.1853. [Cupar g/s]

WALKER, WILLIAM, born 7.5.1830, son of James Walker and Hannah Murray, died in Simcoe, Ontario, 9.8.1900. [Tough g/s]

WALLACE, JANE, daughter of George Wallace {died 1821} and Agnes Gardner {died 1847}, died in New York 1848. [Renfrew, Mearns, g/s]

WALLACE, ROBERT, son of Reverend Robert Wallace {1788-1864} and Elizabeth Smith, died in Mobile aged 44. [Dumfries g/s]

WANN, DAVID, born 1850, son of William Wann and Elizabeth Muir, died in London, Canada West, 22.5.1873. [Monimail g/s]

WARDHAUGH, ANNE, born 1819, widow of George McMichael, died in Newkirk, Oklahoma, 11.10.1904. [Balmaclellan g/s]

WARK, JAMES CLARK, born Paisley 2.2.1829, son of James Wark {1788-1848} a dyer, and Mary Clark {1794-1868}, died in Cincinatti, USA, 29.5.1880. [Paisley, Woodside, g/s]

WATSON, ELIZABETH, born 1780, died in Long Grove, Iowa, 2.12.1866. [West Linton g/s]

WATERS, JAMES, born 1840, died in Boston 26.11.1912. [Stronsay g/s]

WATSON, JAMES, born 1800, son of James Watson {1778-1862} and Elizabeth Mustard {1806-1870}, died in New Orleans 1839. [Broughty Ferry, St Aidan's, g/s]

WATSON, JAMES ANDERSON, born 1882, son of William Watson and Jessie Anderson, died in Boston, Massachusetts, 31.7.1906. [Cambusnethan g/s]

WATSON, JANE, born 1809, died in Welland, Upper Canada, 18.1.1865. [West Linton g/s]

SCOTTISH-AMERICAN GRAVESTONES

WATSON, PETER, born 1858, son of Peter Watson and Janet Paton,
died in Paterson, America, 21.8.1889. [Milnathort g/s]
WATSON, WILLIAM WALLACE, born 20.12.1844, son of James
Loch Watson and Agnes Wallace, died in Montreal 20.11.1903.
[Crosbie g/s]
WATT, CONCEMORE, born 1850, son of Thomas Watt and Esther
Clarke, died in Madison, USA, 14.7.1876. [Edrom g/s]
WATT, JAMES, son of Hugh Watt, a baker in Perth, and Ann Cook,
settled in Charleston, South Carolina, died 19.9.1811. [Perth
Greyfriars g/s]
WATT, JAMES, born 1838, son of George Watt and Helen Meikle,
died in Kansas 29.3.1884. [Dunfermline g/s]
WATT, MAGGIE, born 1861, daughter of William Watt {1831-1864}
a farmer in Hillhead of Auchiries and Mary Chalmers, died in
USA 25.1.1878. [Tyrie g/s]
WEATHERHEAD, CATHERINE, born 1823, wife of James Wilson,
died in Regina, Canada, 30.1.1889. [Newton, Midlothian, g/s]
WEBB, GEORGE, born 1833, died in Victoria, British Columbia,
12.1.1908. [Bellie Tynet g/s]
WEBSTER, ARTHUR, son of Thomas Wenster of Balkeathly, Fife,
{1740-1819}, a merchant in Montreal. [Dundee, Howff, g/s]
WEBSTER, JAMES, born 1809, son of James Webster and Agnes
Hunter, died in Canada 1869. [Liff g/s]
WEBSTER, THOMAS, born 1813, son of James Webster and Agnes
Hunter, died in Arthur, Canada West, 2.10.1857. [Liff g/s]
WEIR, ALEXANDER, borm 1803, son of Alexander Weir and Marion
Smith. died in America 20.6.1885. [Dunsyre g/s]
WEIR, ROBERT, born 1809, son of Robert Weir, a stationer in
Glasgow, and Janet Barry, died in Montreal 10.5.1843.
[Denny g/s]
WEIR, ROBERT, born 1878, son of Robert Weir {1848-1881} and
Maria McKinlay {1852-1879}, died in Texas 1.3.1904.
[Rothesay g/s]
WELSH, DAVID, born 1837, son of David Welsh {1799-1876} and
Jane White {1799-1882}, died in Washington, USA, 26.9.1883.
[Fettercairn g/s]
WELSH, EDWARD, born 1850, died in Nantick, USA, 18.10.1872.
[Parton g/s]

101

WELSH, GEORGE, born 19.7.1811. son of William Welsh and
Elizabeth Sanderson, died in America 6.3.1856.
[Pollockshaws g/s]
WELSH, EDWARD, born 1850, died in Nantick, USA, 18.10.1872.
[Parton g/s]
WELSH, JOHN, son of Thomas Welsh {1779-1836} and Catherine
Biggar {1782-1867}, died in America 6.3.1856.
[Pollockshaws, Kirk Lane, g/s]
WELSH, JOHN, born 1827, son of Walter Welsh, died in Mobile
8.4.1860. [Auchtertool g/s]
WHAMOND, DAVID, born 1822, son of James Whamond and Betty
Wilson, died in Philadelphia 30.4.1874. [Farnell g/s]
WHARRIE, Dr PATRICK SMITH, son of Robert Wharrie of Pathhead
{1748-1818} a surgeon and Elizabeth Smith {1753-1825}, died in
Nelson, Upper Canada, 27.2.1844. [Lesmahagow g/s]
WHITE, THOMAS, son of Andrew White {1769-1841}, settled in
Petersburg, Virginia. [Kirkcaldy g/s]
WHITE, WILLIAM, born 1780, son of David White {1761-1822}
schoolmaster in Duns and Mary Johnston {1743-1798}, died in
Virginia 18.10.1814. [Duns g/s]
WHITELAW, THOMAS, born 1855, son of Robert Whitelaw and
Mary McKean Cunningham, died in Pittsfield, USA, 23.7.1900.
[Alexandria g/s]
WHITLIE, JOHN, born 1800, son of James Whitlie {1766-1837} feuar
in Ayton and Isabel Clark, died in South Trenton, New Jersey,
30.4.1847. [Ayton g/s]
WHITTET, ROBERT, born 1828, son of James Whittet, a painter in
Perth, and Elizabeth Jackson, died 25.8.1908, buried in
Hollywood Cemetery, Richmond, Virginia.
[Perth, Greyfriars, g/s]
WHITTET, THOMAS, born 1840, son of James Whittet, a painter in
Perth, and Elizabeth Jackson, died in Montreal 24.2.1874.
[Perth, Greyfriars, g/s]
WHITTON, WILFED, SMITH, born 8.5.1863, son of Peter Whitton
and Helen Isles, died in Denver, Colorado, 27.7.1900.
[Methven g/s]
WHYTE, AGNES BRYSSON, born 1824, daughter of Robert Whyte
{1778-1851} a merchant, and Agnes Brysson {1787-1847}, wife

102

of James Sneddon a civil engineer in Savannah, Georgia, died
2.12.1854. [Edinburgh, Greyfriars, g/s]

WHYTE, WILLIAM, son of Robert Whyte {1778-1851} a merchant,
and Agnes Brysson {1787-1847}, died in Detroit 18.9.1892.
[Edinburgh, Greyfriars, g/s]

WIGHTON, GEORGE, son of James Wighton {1767-1843} and Jean
Watson {1768-1815}, an engineer in New Orleans.
[Dundee, Old Mains, g/s]

WILKIE, ALEXANDER, born 1797, son of George Wilkie and Jane
Watson, a merchant in Montreal, died in Montreal 21.12.1833.
[Dundee, Howff, g/s]

WILKINS, LORILLA, born in USA 1812, wife of James Wilkins of
Kirkblain, died 20.10.1870. [Dumfries g/s]

WILL, JOHN, born 1811, son of John Will and Elizabeth Stewart
{1789-1854}, died in Montreal 21.6.1832. [Fowlis Easter g/s]

WILL, THOMAS, born 1793, son of Robert Will {1749-1839} a
farmer in Echt and Agnes Thow {1765-1845}, died in Montreal
12.10.1819. [Strachan g/s]

WILLIAMS, or TOUGH, ANN, born 1838, died in Chicago 3.7.1903.
[Dundee, Eastern Necropolis, g/s]

WILLIAMSON, GEORGE, son of Robert Williamson {died 1814} and
Elizabeth Williamson {1780-1860}, died in Carafraxa, Canada
West, 1858. [Banchory Tiernan g/s]

WILLIAMSON, JOHN, of Meiklour, born 1801, 'late of New York',
died in Blairgowrie 9.8.1871. [Lethendy g/s]

WILLIAMSON, MARGARET, born 1831, wife of Daniel Stewart,
died in Apaculpo, Mexico, 3.9.1853.
[Kirkcaldy, Abbotshall, g/s]

WILSON, ALEXANDRINA, daughter of J. & M. Wilson, died in
Virginia 16.8.1880. [Duddingston g/s]

WILSON, ANDREW, born 1784, son of John Wilson {1747-1787} and
Margaret Blythe {1750-1829}, died in New York 1.9.1832.
[Dunbar g/s]

WILSON, JAMES, a merchant in Charleston, South Carolina, died
27.12.1823. [Crieff g/s]

WILSON, JAMES, born 1823, late farmer in Newton, Midlothian,
husband of Catherine Weatherfield, died in McLeod, Canada,
5.8.1899. [Newton g/s]

WILSON, JAMES JACK, son of James L. Wilson and Annie
Brownlee, died in Ingersoll, Canada, 30.1.1881. [Carluke g/s]
WILSON, JOHN, born in Edinburgh 1800, a vocalist, died in Quebec
8.7.1849. [Edinburgh, Dean, g/s]
WILSON, MARY, born 1794, wife of Robert Hamilton, died in
Argyle, Lafayette County, Wisconsin, 13.5.1868.
[Carsphairn g/s]
WILSON, MATILDA S., born 1848, died 1928, buried in Boston,
Massachusetts. [Brechin Cathedral g/s]
WILSON, THOMAS, born 1763, son of Robert Wilson {1737-1782}
and Alison Darling, died in Philadelphia 26.1.1830.
[Preston, Berwickshire, g/s]
WILSON, THOMAS H., son of John Wilson {1805-1869} and
Margaret Hood {1815-1908}, settled in Eaton, Colorado.
[Lintrathen g/s]
WISHART, Reverend THOMAS, born 9.6.1809, died in St John, New
Brunswick, 12.1.1853. [Edinburgh, Greyfriars, g/s]
WISHART, PHILADELPHIA ANNE, born 13.2.1814, wife of
William MacNider MD in Montreal, died 29.10.1890.
[Edinburgh, Greyfriars, g/s]
WITHERSPOON, JOHN, born in Yester 5.2.1723, son of Reverend
James Witherspoon, President of Princeton College, New Jersey,
Member of Congress, and Signatory of the Declaration of
Independence, died in USA 15.11.1794. [Yester, Gifford, g/s]
WOOD, THOMAS, born 1759, son of James Wood and Margaret
Barclay, died in America 1818. [Fetteresso g/s]
WOODWARD, RUFUS, born 16.7.1793 in Torringford, Connecticut,
graduated from Yale University 1816, died in Edinburgh
24.11.1823. [St Cuthbert's, Edinburgh, g/s]
WRIGHT, ANDREW, born 1835, son of Duncan Wright and Helen
Baird, died in New York 1.2.1873. [Tulliallan g/s]
WYLLIE, ALEXANDER, born 1825, son of John Wyllie and
Margaret Conning, died in Savanna 7.1.1852. [Borgue g/s]
WYLLIE, ALEXANDER, born 1843, son of Robert Wyllie and
Elizabeth Soutar, died in Cedar Forest, Virginia, 10.11.1899.
[Brechin g/s]
WYLLIE, JAMES, soldier of C Company of the 1st Michigan Cavalry,
died in the US Civil War 1861-1865.

[Old Calton, Edinburgh, g/s]

WYLIE, ROBERT C., son of Alexander Wylie {1762-1840} and Janet Creighton {1766-1847}, a merchant in Mazathon, Mexico. [Dunlop g/s]

WYLIE, WILLIAM, son of Reverend John Wylie {1793-1873} and Caroline Ann Dick {1803-1876}, died in the St Lawrence River 7.5.1859. [Carluke g/s]

YEAMAN, JAMES, born in Oathlaw 15.9.1845, son of Robert Yeaman and Susan Scott, "sometime in California", died in Dundee 1.12.1906. [Oathlaw g/s]

YOUNG, JAMES, born 1799, son of Alexander Young and Joan Quarrier Broxburn, died in Richmond, Virginia, 2.8.1815. [Uphall g/s]

YOUNG, JAMES, born 1849, son of John Young of Dovehill {1819-1852} and Margaret Arthur {1823-1903}, died in Metcalfe, Canada, 27.6.1901. [Caputh g/s]

YOUNG, JOHN, son of James Young a merchant in Galston and Margaret Mason {1784-1811}, settled in Hamilton, Ontario. [Loudoun g/s]

YOUNG, MARY, born 1793, wife of James Faulds, died in New York 8.10.1835. [Dundee, Howff, g/s]

YOUNG, ROBERT, born 1844, son of James Young and Margaret Martin, died in Tacoma, USA, 31.1.1889. [Montrose, Rosehill, g/s]

YOUNG, THOMAS, born 1845, died in Joplin, Missouri, 5.9.1873. [Dunlop g/s]

YOUNG, WILLIAM B., born 1856, son of James Young and Fanny Turton, died in California 2.3.1903. [Blairgowrie g/s]

YULE, JAMES, son of John Yule {1764-1839} a farmer in Craigievar and Elizabeth Cooper {1770-1812}, settled in USA. [Leochel g/s]